"Much in this book is how I try to approach the game with my players. The idea of 'sucking less' is so true, as you fail much more than you succeed in this game—which, for a kid, teaches you how to deal with failure and rid yourself of that 'stinkin' thinkin'' that so many carry with them."

Joey Hale

Coach of the 2012 Little League World Series Champions
(and 2015 runner up), Goodlettsville, TN

"I'm so excited to see *Swing for the Fences* . . . it's fabulous and right in line with books that dad and I are passionate about."

Anita Oliva

Owner and Business Consultant, Oliva Management LLC, M Design Interactive Inc.

Tony Oliva

Former star outfielder, batting champion, and All-Star for the Minnesota Twins

"As a baseball coach and a father of two boys who love baseball, *Swing for the Fences* reinforces my feeling that baseball is a great teacher of the game of life. The life lessons learned, from dealing with failures to relationships, provide an essential tool for young men to cope with the ever-changing world around them."

Ryan Folmar

Head Coach, Oral Roberts University baseball, Tulsa, OK

"An American pastime, baseball's roots can be traced to ancient religious rituals. Greg Bancroft mines these depths, and demonstrates how the dynamics of baseball's wisdom can apply to living a fulfilling life."

The Rt. Rev. Mark Beckwith

Bishop of the Episcopal Diocese of Newark
and ardent Red Sox fan

"The game of baseball is filled with stories of inspirational leaders, both in the dugout and on the field. *Swing for the Fences* illustrates how the examples set by them can be applied to everyday life."

Bob Showers

Author of *Twins in the Dome, Twins at the Met,*
and *Minnesota North Stars*

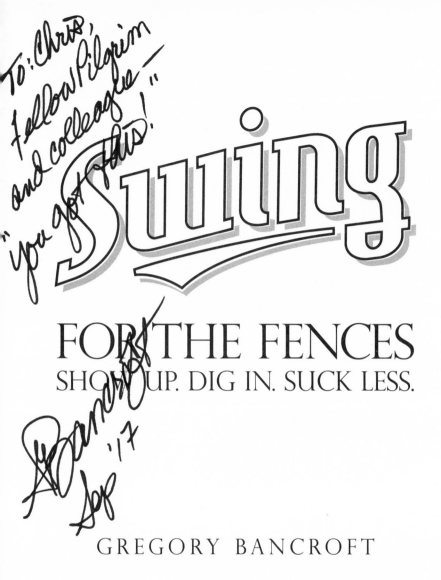

FOR THE FENCES

SHOW UP. DIG IN. SUCK LESS.

GREGORY BANCROFT

WISE *Ink*
CREATIVE ★ PUBLISHING

To: Chris, fellow Pilgrim and colleague "you got this!"

Bancroft '17 Sep

ISBN 13: 978-1-63489-940-6
eISBN: 978-1-63489-939-0

Library of Congress Catalog Number: 2017933036
Printed in the United States of America
First Printing: 2017

21 20 19 18 17   5 4 3 2 1

Cover and interior design:
Rick Korab, Korab Company Design

*A portion of the proceeds from this book will go
to support youth softball and baseball programs*

Wise Ink Creative Publishing
837 Glenwood Ave.
Minneapolis, MN 55405
www.wiseinkpub.com

To order, visit www.itascabooks.com or call
1-800-901-3480. Reseller discounts available.

To my wife, Sally

TABLE OF CONTENTS

CHAPTER 1

SWING FOR THE FENCES:
Embrace Failure

"Sticks and stones may break my bones, but words will never hurt me," goes the childhood meme that we all learned in school. That's what we were supposed to say to someone who taunted us with shaming epithets like "loser," "fake," "dork." Over time, our scratches, bruises, and even our broken bones did heal. Yet, those taunting words still echo in our consciousness. Left unchallenged, those words fester and become "stinkin' thinkin'." We don't need an older brother around, telling us what losers we are. We have built-in sound systems that reverberate in our brains, repeating over and over again that we don't measure up. We suck. No matter how hard we try, we are just not quite good enough. It's not that we have done something wrong or that we are bad people. It's just that we always seem to fall short of the goal.

That stinkin' thinkin' is more pervasive in our culture than we'd like to believe. It's time for a revolution. Rather than a call to arms, I'm suggesting a "call to bats." Let's use the lessons of base-ball, especially a "swing-for-the-fences" mentality, to overcome the shaming messages bouncing around in our heads. Our fences are out there. They are the deepest hopes, long-held dreams, great passions, and strongest desires of our hearts. We would love nothing better than to connect with and hit the sweet-spot response to some situation in our lives that allows us to knock it out of the park. We could touch all the bases and jump on home plate while those around us cheer. We could say to those old voices, "be gone," and create new voices that affirm us, accept us, love us. We could be the people we were meant to be.

Who wakes up in the morning intending to fail? Who plans to screw up everything at work, sabotage every project, say hurtful words to people, and generally ruin every attempted human interaction? Let's say no one, even though there could be some really sick people who do just that. But we know lots of people—in our families, schools, and places of worship—who love to tell us how we constantly fail to measure up. No matter how hard we've tried, it is just never good enough. Well, guess what? We DO fail more times than we succeed! Lots more. So, let's embrace failure! Let's embrace baseball as a way to overcome the stinkin' thinkin' that so often immobilizes us and makes us feel so terrible.

That's right. Baseball. It's a game of failure. It's also about teamwork, sacrifice, affirmation, grace, tolerance, and a whole bunch more. Learn the lessons of baseball, and you will navigate the sticks, stones, and awful words slung in your direction. Remember that baseball is the only sport where the person scores, not the ball . . . and the person comes "home" to do so. You are more important than any "thing," and others are counting on you. Of course, you'll suck. Baseball is not about perfection. You just need to suck less. You do that by showing up every day, digging into what you have to do, and swinging for the fences. You'll practice. Your attitude and effort will pay off—just not all the time. Get really involved in the game of baseball, and you'll see a whole new ontology (the way things are in the universe) unfold before you. It starts with hitting.

The hardest thing to do in all of sports is to hit a round ball with a round bat. The ball is often spinning and traveling at close to 100 miles per hour, taking less than half a second to reach the batter. The sweet spot on the round-surfaced bat, which is swinging toward the ball, is the size of a dime. To hit that ball and make it travel to anywhere on the field in a manner that someone won't catch it, scoop it up, or throw it to a base is ridiculously hard. Doing so successfully three times out of ten (yielding a slightly better than .300 batting average) would probably land a person a Major League contract. Ted Williams, the greatest hitter of all time, entered the Baseball Hall of Fame with a career batting average of .344 and finished one season with slightly over .400 (read: four hundred). Where in life can you FAIL six or even seven times out of ten and still be richly rewarded?

To be sure, all hitters practice in the batting cage. Hundreds of balls come at them, sometimes at great speed, and they hit virtually every one of them. But in a game, things are different. Not all pitchers throw the same way. Oftentimes, a curve ball comes unexpectedly, and the batter's concentration is disrupted. The batter cannot guarantee success, even with all the practice in the world. However, the batter will most certainly guarantee failure by not swinging the bat. Focusing on how many times they missed the ball or how poorly the time at bat went is not what puts batters into the Baseball Hall of Fame. It is how many times the batter came to the plate, dug in, and swung for the fences that maybe, just maybe, resulted in his scoring a run, winning a game, or even just getting to stand on first base for a while.

Get your bat off your shoulder. Embrace failure. Swing for the fences. ❤

In the Batter's Box

Consider your own stinkin' thinkin.' On this page, write whose voice/s you hear. What are they saying? In what way/s can you step up to the plate, dig in, and suck less? Describe what it would be like to swing for the fences. How does that feel?

CHAPTER 2

IT ALL STARTS WITH LITTLE LEAGUE:
Absorb Affirmation

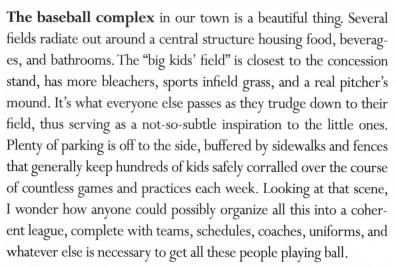

The baseball complex in our town is a beautiful thing. Several fields radiate out around a central structure housing food, beverages, and bathrooms. The "big kids' field" is closest to the concession stand, has more bleachers, sports infield grass, and a real pitcher's mound. It's what everyone else passes as they trudge down to their field, thus serving as a not-so-subtle inspiration to the little ones. Plenty of parking is off to the side, buffered by sidewalks and fences that generally keep hundreds of kids safely corralled over the course of countless games and practices each week. Looking at that scene, I wonder how anyone could possibly organize all this into a coherent league, complete with teams, schedules, coaches, uniforms, and whatever else is necessary to get all these people playing ball.

Volunteers. Dozens of volunteers. Dozens of moms and dads herd squirrely kids to their respective fields. They group them into gaggles of loud, laughing, pushing units soon to become teams, complete with distinctive T-shirts and caps uniting them as tribes. At least for a season, these kids will be bound together as they win or lose games, practice fundamental drills, and learn the basics of the greatest game ever invented. Some will continue to play together all the way to the big kids' field. Others will drop out along the way. But for a time, they will belong to something larger than themselves. They will learn the value of teamwork while supporting and encouraging one another. Tolerance, patience, and acceptance will become such a part of their shared experience that soon they will naturally wait while a teammate struggles through all fifteen pitches before running to first base. Yelling support and encouragement to one another will become second nature as their cheers propel the runners around the bases. Words like "good eye," "good cut," "nice throw," "way to hustle," make up the marinating sauce of affirmation that saturates a Little League game. I once saw two teams of softball players file out to the shortstop who had just caught a fly ball. All the girls patted her on the back for a job well done. Lining up for the high five at the end of the game is one of the highlights of the entire Little League experience. Win or lose, our team congratulates your team on a game well played.

"Always go to other people's funerals, otherwise they won't come to yours," Yogi Berra is quoted saying. Over the years, as a parish priest and counselor, as well as in various business settings, I have witnessed how people have become increasingly disconnected from one another. The bonds that once held our society together, such as church attendance, engagement in civic activities, and even league bowling, have all seen a decline in participation over the last forty years or more. Add in long commutes, multiple jobs, and frequent relocations and it's little wonder the old bonds connecting us to one another have frayed. I hear over and over again how no one has any time for anything, let alone something that might actually improve mental, spiritual, or psychological well-being. Compounding this malaise is the fact that it is rare to find a person who is marinating in affirmation at work, school, or elsewhere.

Meanwhile, as Little Leaguers mature, the cheering and encouragement never stops. Affirmations of "good swing," "nice throw," "way to go," are constantly raining down on everyone, nurturing the kind of environment that so richly describes baseball. Kids learn to back up throws and pat each other on the back after a scored run or how to offer words of encouragement after someone strikes out. An errant throw or a called third strike is taken in stride because the next such occurrence could be one's own. Kids show up, dig in, and swing for the fences because their teammates need them to do so. Kids demonstrate tolerance, acceptance, patience, and constant encouragement because it's what keeps everyone going strong. Fans lose themselves in the activity and come away strangely refreshed. Imagine being immersed in a non-shaming environment where the only purpose is to run around touching three canvas bags and jumping on a funny-shaped rubber plate while people constantly shout uplifting comments to one another . . .

A key message of Little League is this: be yourself. You are fine just the way you are. Everyone can swing a bat, catch a ball, throw a ball, run the bases, and—most importantly—cheer on teammates. There are no superstars in baseball. It takes a whole team playing every day to have a winning season. It takes everyone showing up, digging in, and swinging for the fences. And sucking less. You'll get better at the fundamentals the more you play. You'll never be perfect—that's impossible. And, in baseball, celebrated! Hitting safely three times out of ten is just fine.

Notice the expressions of support and encouragement are directed at behavior, not personality. People are intrinsically valuable, worthwhile, and precious. Overcoming the toxic nature of our shame-based culture requires little steps, made consistently and relentlessly. The constant chatter of "way to go" is easy to do, doesn't cost anything, can be done by anyone, and becomes second nature the more we do it. It's central to the lessons we learned way back in Little League where everyone shows up, digs in, and swings for the fences. Over time, we'll suck less and less. Over time, our human bonds will strengthen, and we'll feel more connected, more a part of a tribe, and—who knows—discover a more caring community sprouting up all around us. ♥

In the Batter's Box

List a few ways that you could practice a Little League experience at home, work, school, or your place of worship. Consciously work at saying only affirming words every day for two weeks with those around you. Record your observations and your feelings. How are you adjusting your thinking in order to say only affirming words? How did that experiment feel along the way? How about after two weeks?

It All Starts With Liitle League: Absorb Affirmation

CHAPTER 3

SPRING TRAINING:
Reinforce Learnings

People often wonder why professional athletes would need a month (or more, if you're a pitcher) to get ready for a full, regular season of baseball. Haven't these people been playing ball since they were five years old? Did they play last year? Are they likely to learn something new over the next few weeks that they do not already know? The answer may surprise some people.

New players appear. They were acquired through trades conducted during the off-season, drafted in the regular rounds, or they're walk-ons hoping for a spot on this season's roster. Everybody, from a walk-on to the Most Valuable Player from last year's team, must bring his A game and work hard to earn (or re-earn) his position on this year's squad. Over time, even the most talented players slow down; age takes its toll. Cal Ripken, Jr. of the Baltimore Orioles played nearly every inning of every game for twenty years—simply an amazing feat in any sport. However, even Cal ran out of steam one year and was replaced, though he had the sense and grace to retire before being ignominiously booted from the team.

Like learning multiplication tables, any life skill (especially any sports skill) takes time. We all know how to swing a bat or throw a ball. We have seen that activity, at the very least, and perhaps have done it a few times, even if we have not played baseball regularly. Likewise, we all know how to listen to a spouse, encourage a child struggling with math, or support a coworker on a project. We are in this game of life together. Having a "we" attitude rather than a "me" attitude is what will strengthen all of our relationships with family, friends, community, work, and country. It will help us "reclaim the commons," those things in life that belong to us all, from our environment to our democracy to our way of life. It's a "swing-for-the-fences" attitude.

Essential to spring training is exercising key muscles, not resting on last year's performance, and keeping oneself activated and motivated. That's why there is great excitement surrounding spring training. Players, coaches, and fans all ask, "Who are we going to be this year?" It's a metaphor for addressing the perennial quest of couples, families, work teams, and communities. How can we build on our past, use our strengths, and be the best we can be this year? Folks from northern climates who come to spring training games are euphoric. Wearing shorts and sandals takes them away from the snow and ice, transporting them to the promise of summer. The constant chatter ("good eye," "good cut," "way to hustle") sounds like Little League as affirming memories wash over them.

Spring training camp is the closest thing adults have to Little League. A player digs in at the plate after awkwardly missing a nasty slider, knowing that his job may depend on getting a hit. Surely, his team's chances of winning in the regular season may very well rest on his ability to hit such a pitch in a clutch situation. He knows what to do. He just has to suck less at doing it. The constant chatter of positive encouragement is good practice before the games are truly on the line. He knows that his team members rely on him, just as he relies on them, to swing for the fences.

Spring training is an opportunity to make Little League as real and dynamic as it was when players were ten years old. And it happens every single year. Baseball is a game of fundamentals—catching a fly ball with two hands, putting a knee down to catch a ground ball, lifting the bat off one's shoulder to be able to swing away, and watching the coach for a sign to steal a base. Getting excited about the game again happens every year at spring training. Having new people around gives everyone a chance to show their skills at team building. When individuals work hard to earn a spot on that team, it motivates players who want to identify with the group and be part of something larger than themselves. It's exciting to see teammates committed to being the best they can be and to see them show up to the tasks at hand, dig in to face any challenge, and suck less at what they already know how to do as they swing for the fences. But it's also a metaphor for life.

Every spring training experience is an opportunity to recall and regroup (think of New Year's resolutions, annual planning meetings, welcoming new team members, marriage, divorce, death, a new baby, work restructuring, and more). Recognize the past and the learning that we can garner from what transpired last time. Come together to motivate and activate one another. In ways small or great, we are a new team, even a new family or work group, on a regular basis. Like every spring training experience, with players showing up to put forth their best efforts, encourage each other, and work for the common good, we can coalesce into a team that is ready to take on the long-haul season of living in the modern world. And that season begins with Opening Day! ♥

In the Batter's Box

What are some spring training experiences in your life from the past five years? How have you worked with others to create a Little League experience (marinating in affirmation)? If it was not a positive Little League experience, revisit it with others to recall the learnings from the past and regroup as a team. What would have to happen for that learning to become a reality? How would things change for you and for others? How would that feel?

CHAPTER 4

OPENING DAY:
Revisit Hope

My team did not win the World Series last year. They could, this year. Although, nothing in the past decade indicates that that's remotely possible . . . so what? At this point in the season, before any games are played, before anyone gets injured, before any trades are executed, my team has every chance that yours does. Even if your team won the Series last year. Didn't my team beat the winners of a World Series in a Spring Training game? So what if that team fielded their bottom-tier players in order to prevent injury to their starters or to give them a day off? The logic of this matters not. The fact remains: my not-so-good team beat the best. This translates into hope for the coming season, even if one must apply syllogistic reasoning to make the case. The illusion of equal footing is only part of the appeal of Opening Day. New life, rebirth, hope, and anticipation are over-arching themes of any baseball fan's ontology, or explanation of the meaning of life.

In addition to anticipation, Opening Day sets the tone for the rest of the season. Who shows up? Do the players of spring training who gave their all and displayed the team-building qualities of Little League come to play? Who are the leaders in the clubhouse, on the bench, and in the field? Do we hear the language of Little League— the positive chatter, encouragement, and non-judgmental support? And what of the coaches? Do they have the never-say-die attitude of a winner? Do they inspire the players to work together for the sake of the team? How about the fans? Are we wide-eyed believers?

Could this be "the year"? Before we become cynical and dispirited, could we hope against hope that the team players running to their places for the first time this season really represent the best of all our hopes and dreams? What if this is a 175-game season unfolding before us? What if we make the playoffs and "go all the way" to the World Series?

People want to believe. We want to be associated with success and winning. We want to put faith into something that will pull us out of ourselves—something to which we can direct our attention. We want something that will reflect that success back onto us. It's silly, maybe. How in the world are you a better person than me simply because your team won the World Series last year? But sports fans, if not most people, allow that reflected glory to define them in a positive light somehow. Maybe it shows good judgment if people throw their allegiance to a winning team. Whatever the psychology, identifying with a winning team makes a lot of people feel better. We know intellectually that we are not defined by our actions or the actions of others. We are intrinsically valuable just because. We are not what we do (or don't do); we are who we are (a gift to the universe).

Nevertheless, Opening Day is important on several levels. As a harbinger of the coming season, it shows us the strength of the team. How well does the team exhibit the fundamentals of Little League, especially the constant positive chatter, mutual respect, tolerance, grace, and forgiveness? The coach or manager becomes very important. That's the person who will take what's "here" and turn it into a winning season—or not. But leadership does not just rest with the one holding the title. Leadership comes from people who lead.

Keeping one's spirits up at work or during a 162-game season takes work. Having a practical joker in the locker room or someone with a lighthearted attitude in the dugout is often the elixir that brightens a batter in the midst of a slump, helps a team shake off a tough loss, or overcomes someone's self-defeating mindset in the face of a dominating pitcher. The leader is the one who leads the team out of the dumps and back into the swing-for-the-fences posture of spring training. And, just like on the ball field, the intangibles of personality and the ability to engage one's teammates at work are often what create an inspiring culture or one that leads to people looking elsewhere after a short tenure. Likewise, a dreaded manager or a "Debbie Downer" often leads to low productivity, dissatisfaction on the job, and constant staff turnover.

On Opening Day, we get to see the team's culture. We witness the chemistry of players and coaches. We gain a sense of who the leaders are on and off the field. Our hopes soar as we envision this team. This year seems like "the one." Or we slink back into our seats as we realize it's the same old uninspired group we saw last year. It is not always about the star quality of players, either. I remember the year the Minnesota Twins beat the New York Mets in spring training—their first-tier players. There was something electric about the guys on the field and in the dugout. That electricity sparkled all season long. The Twins had a slightly better than .500 season, losing just a few less games than they won. Tom Kelly, the manager that year, took what he had and coached them to a World Series Championship. Average by the numbers, they worked together as a team, truly a Little League team with all its positive attributes as they swung for the fences every day. It was clear on Opening Day, as they charged out to their places, as they chattered and encouraged and supported each other, that this team was special. Clearly, their specialness was not because of the numbers. It came from the intangibles, from the leadership of the players and a coach who inspired them to show up, dig in, and suck less. They did so in spring training and on Opening Day. They continued throughout the long-haul season . . . and beyond.

We know what to do. Show up every day with the mindset and

the attitude of being at spring training. It's about bringing Little League to life again and again. Rebirth. Dig into the tasks at hand. Your team, family, and neighbors count on you, and you count on them. Suck less. We are not talking about perfection. We're talking about constancy, lifting the bat of indifference, laziness, fear, or whatever else holds you back, and actually swinging for the fences. Hope. Anticipate good things happening. You can't guarantee success, but you can guarantee failure if you just stand there. Swinging away, day in and day out, at work, home, school, or on the baseball field is the long-haul struggle we all face. Make the most of that struggle and live into the joy you know to be the game of baseball. ♥

In the Batter's Box

What is your biggest hope? Are there regularly occurring situations at home or work where you anticipate something good? How can you bring the positive attitude of Little League and the underpinnings of spring training to bear on those situations and create the promise of an Opening Day? How would that feel?

CHAPTER 5

THE LONG-HAUL SEASON:
Persevere Persistently

In the 1920s, there were sixteen teams split between two leagues. Every team played its rival teams eleven times at home and eleven times away (twenty-two games total per rival) for a 154-game season. Then, both leagues expanded and decided that playing eighteen games per rival was satisfactory—and the 162-game season became the norm. Later, divisions within leagues were created, interleague play developed and soon there was the specter of 198 game season, if the practice of the past continued. Yet, 162 games had been the standard for a generation. No team wanted to give up home games because of the revenue (sales) involved. Not too many people wanted to add games and go into November for World Series games (potentially too cold). So, the number of 162 games remained. A long season, by any definition.

162 games equals (using a rough average) 1,458 innings, 4,374 outs, 24,300 pitches thrown, 2,916 hits, 324 home runs, 2,268 strikeouts, 1,134 walks, and an astonishing 16,200 baseballs used. It's anyone's guess how many gallons of beer are consumed or the thousands of hotdogs and brats that get chomped. Add in fans, media personalities, field workers, parking lot attendants, food servers, and so on, and the numbers are staggering. However, for the most part, it's the players, coaches, and to some extent, media personalities who must persevere through the long-haul season of Major League Baseball. I listen to a great many games on the radio. I watch my fair share on TV. I go to a lot of games. Yet, as diehard a fan

as I am, I don't persevere through nearly 1,500 innings of baseball every year. It's one thing to show up, dig in, and swing for the fences during the hustle of spring training or the excitement of Opening Day. It's a whole different ball game to do so for an entire season. Just imagine 1,458 innings . . .

Maintaining a Little League culture becomes increasingly difficult as players enter slumps. Traveling around the country grows tedious, and irritating personal quirks begin to grate on one another's nerves. In any relationship, the mountaintop experiences are fun and exciting. With so many things going right, it's easy to overlook what's wrong and just enjoy the high.

During times of struggle, like severe illness, natural disaster, or major life changes, even the weakest of partners can muster the courage and strength necessary to prevail—at least for a time.

Rather, it's the day-in, day-out routine that forms relationships and determines their success. If the fundamentals are in place, if the marinating words of affirmation are the first language of all involved; if there is a sense of hope, anticipation, and adventure about the future, then people will produce a steadfastness of purpose. Tenacity will take root, which will create a determined, never-say-die attitude in the team, family, or couple. An indefatigable spirit will be the hallmark of their interactions with the world, despite delay or failure in achieving success. And it's not about getting through the flat times until we get to another mountaintop high. It's also not about finding tricks or diversions to avoid the valleys. We don't endure the flat times like a road trip across the prairie. It's all of a piece, and our best option is to pull up our socks, wipe our noses, and soldier on.

Baseball is terribly routine. Every day there are basics to drill, time in the batting cage to complete, equipment and uniforms to maintain, as well as fields to prepare. And at the same time, each game is unique, special, and meaningful in some way to someone.

I've seen people get engaged at games, kids go crazy chasing a foul ball, spouses kiss on giant screens, babies asleep in a blanket at their first game, and grandpas help grandchildren learn how to score a game—a memory that will stick with those kids their whole lives. Tonight's game might be the one where only the twenty-eighth player in Major League history hit for the cycle. More likely, it's the one where friends realize just how much their lives are enriched by each other's companionship, even if they never say so.

A long-married couple in one of my past parishes illustrates how to persevere persistently. They never used harsh language about anyone or anything, especially not while talking with each other. Graceful, hopeful, and affirming words attended all their conversations. It was clear when they were mad or displeased, even with each other. But the first language used was positive. They did not sweat the small stuff. They had seen their share of trials and tribulations and had survived great tragedies. Nothing was the end of the world except the end of the world. Setting the table, a task performed thousands of times between them, was an exercise in grace. No words. Simple motions. Mission accomplished. They anticipated the future, looked forward to new adventures, even though the vast majority of their days looked pretty much the same as far as I could tell. There was constancy, a steadfastness about them that created a sense of assurance among the rest of us blessed to have them in our lives. The world is good. We'll be okay. ❧

In the Batter's Box

You've been practicing the language of Little League at work or school. Hopefully, you use that language with the person closest to you. One tragedy of being rooted in a shame-based culture is the toxic noise clogging our thoughts that some call "arrival psychology." This is the sense that a current situation must be endured until things improve. "I'll be okay when I graduate," "I'll be okay if I get married by next summer" . . . if . . . when. Where do you have arrival psychology? What can you tell yourself about the value of routine without yearning for the high of a mountaintop moment or the drama of a valley experience? How does it feel to persevere persistently?

CHAPTER 6

SHOW UP, DIG IN:
Control Attitude

I'm an ardent fan of outdoor baseball. You can't control the weather. Some games are played in scorching heat and humidity and others while skies threaten rain. I've seen a SNOW delay (it was snowing so hard, the batter couldn't see the ball, and the pitcher could barely see his catcher). I've also witnessed a game delay due to the presence of bees. Yep, bees. One of my favorite sensations is the scent of freshly mowed grass twisting through the air with a mixture of grilled burgers and onion rings on the wind when it's about seventy degrees. Although external factors can make watching a game more or less comfortable, my overall experience starts with how I enter the ballpark. Am I excited to be there? Is this the game when I finally catch a foul ball (it's been fifty years or more)? Who will be the team leader for this game? Do I want a brat or a chilidog?

I come early. I like to get my scorebook filled out with the day's roster. I like to see the pregame activity: batters swinging, players running, balls flying around, and coaches talking to media. I can toss down a cool one and devour a meat-like treat while watching the setup for today's game. Then, when the opening pitch is delivered, I am totally ready. I always have a positive attitude going to a game, and I am always ready—or nearly so.

Attitude. Great expressions surround this condition. One of my favorite posters is of a guy whose nose resembles a tap dispensing lemonade while his head is a funnel with dozens of lemons pouring into it. The caption is, of course, "When life gives you lemons, make lemonade." You've heard someone say, "I'm a glass-half-full kind of person." This means that no matter what the situation is, this person sees the positive and focuses on the good. While not ignoring the bad or difficult, this glass-half-full person is driven by the possible in that situation. Likewise, we all know people who constantly harp on the negative. Nothing ever seems quite satisfactory. Everything could be better. Criticism curls out of their mouths at every corner. Not only is it difficult to be around such people, it's actually unhealthy for our hearts and toxic to our well-being. Clearly, a glass-half-empty person is plagued with another form of stinkin' thinkin.' So imagine how terrible it would be for a glass-half-empty player to be coursing through the dugout, spewing negativity, focusing on how nothing is good enough, the umpires are against him, and the crummy weather. It happens. Teams suffer.

Glass-half-empty people abound in our culture. We encounter them at school, on work teams, at places of worship, and even within our families. We all suffer. Productivity is lost. Teaching is hampered. Our spirits lag. We dread holidays. No matter what I say or what I do, I cannot change that person's attitude. I can't turn that person into a glass-half-full person. I can point out his or her behavior and challenge the person's thinking, risking an argument and further deterioration of the situation. Or, I can leave (physically or psychologically). Which is to say, I can engage or not. And this is where teams fall apart, work becomes disjointed, learning falters, and people stop coming to worship.

Fundamental to the game of baseball is one's attitude. Psychologists talk about "faking it until making it" in terms of recovery from addiction. That is, we can become what we think about. Focusing our attention is key to health and well-being. "Think like a winner" becomes "act like a winner," and performance improves. Attitude is so critical that some sports teams hire psychologists, motivational speakers, and even chaplains to help people adjust their thinking to a positive frame of mind. However, simply thinking positively will not make you a great ball player. As we'll see in the next chapter, you have to control your effort and practice, practice, practice. But you first have to show up, physically and mentally, have a positive attitude, and be ready. Dig into the task at hand. Focus. Concentrate. Be there for your team. Decide that you want to be here (in this marriage, part of this family, a member of this worshipping body, or a player on this team).

You can control your thinking and attitude and decide to be positive. You can look for the possible in any situation. Keep that attitude from Little League spring training and Opening Day alive. You can dig into whatever you are about to confront (a Cy Young Award-winning pitcher, your grumpy uncle, or your daughter's chemistry homework). You have to get in the game to be in the game. Show up and dig in. You can't play from the stands. You'll have to be ready, of course. You might have to do some advance planning. Baseball teams review films that show how tomorrow's opposing pitcher is likely to approach the game. They notice the pitch sequence and see that a curve often follows a series of sliders. The pitch is designed to keep batters off balance and tentative—all the more reason to prepare, show up, dig in, and swing for the fences. Preparation is important. The beauty of baseball is actually how unpredictable it can be. Even with preparation, you have to be flexible to remain positive.

You have heard people say that life threw them a real curveball. There's the middle-aged man who was laid off from a job he held for more than twenty years, with zero notice. The woman who discovered a lump and spent the next three years in a battle for her life. Having a positive attitude is what got both of these people through the unexpected, the terrifying, the long-haul season of a difficult life experience. Neither one could change the situation. Both wished for something different. What they could do, they did. They controlled their attitudes. Both people made it through their ordeals by showing up, digging in, and swinging for the fences. ♥

In the Batter's Box

Where are you in need of an attitude adjustment? You practiced saying
something positive about other people (see chapter two). Now, practice
thinking only positive thoughts for the next two weeks. Look for the
possible in some situation at home, your office, school, or wherever else
might need some Little League positivity. Apply this approach first in
your thinking and then in your actions. Note how you feel. What's different about you? About the people around you? Has anything changed to
make things better? How has this approach altered any stinkin' thinkin'
you might harbor?

CHAPTER 7

SUCK LESS:
Control Effort

Michael Jordan is often considered one of the best basketball players of all time. No doubt about it, he was phenomenal. How many games did he win for the Chicago Bulls? How often was he the leader of his team, emotionally and physically? Lots. Did you know that he didn't even make his high school team? He wasn't that good. He got cut. So, as we saw in the last chapter, Michael adjusted his attitude by focusing on the positive, seeing the possible, and he did what he had to do—practice. Other than his attitude, the only thing he could really control was his effort. That effort changed his life.

Natural talent aside, practice will obviously improve anyone's results. Of course, you have to practice the right skills and develop the right habits, since doing the opposite will just compound the problem and lack of success. Fortunately for baseball players, they don't have to be Michael Jordan. If they can just be consistently good enough in the batter's box (say, three out of ten times), they stand a chance of helping any team. Any team saturated with Little League affirmation, that is.

Do you love those dramatic outfield catches where the guy runs full tilt, and at the last moment, stretches out completely to snag the ball in his glove (often called a Superman catch)? How about the ballet-beautiful double play performed by a second baseman and a shortstop who have played together and practiced together for years? You know the ones. The second baseman lurches to his right and slaps the ball with his glove in a time-saving gesture to get it to the shortstop, now gliding over the bag, who grabs it with his throwing hand as he leaps over the runner and throws to first in time to get the recent batter. All these instances demonstrate effort. It's the one thing that individuals can control. When a whole team decides to put forth the effort, you see the totally-focused-gotta-get-it-done kind of effort just described. It's a rewarding experience. Win or lose, as a player or fan, it is very exciting to be a part of such effort.

A pitcher in the Major League spends hours on simple mechanics. Holding the ball, stepping toward home plate a certain way, pushing his rear leg at just the right time, and focusing on an area the size of a shoebox sixty feet away, he releases the pitch—a pitch now subject to the elements of weather and physics. He practices each pitch, with all its subtle vagaries of mechanics, thousands of times. In the National League, the pitcher will also spend a few moments in the batting cage. This is because they come to bat in the National League whereas pitchers in the American League are spared embarrassment at the plate by virtue of the designated hitter.

Everyone else practices throwing, catching, running bases, and sliding into second and whatnot. They spend a great majority of their time swinging at balls. Thousands and thousands of balls will come hurtling toward you if you play baseball long enough. Players will never master how to swing at them productively. You'll get better, never perfect. You can't control the pitch, the weather, or the umpire's call, and you can't alter physics. You cannot guarantee success if you swing your bat. You will, however, guarantee failure if you leave the bat on your shoulder. After you have controlled your attitude (be positive, see the possible), you can control your effort. You showed up. You dug in. Now swing. Suck less, with practice. But swing.

So why don't more people swing for the fences in life? Perhaps they have the stinkin' thinkin' of shame reverberating in their brains. All they hear is that they are not quite good enough, and they don't measure up. Or perhaps they have the stinkin' thinkin' of negativity curdling in their veins. Everything is awful. They turned their mouths upside down and can't get them right side up again. Maybe they are afflicted with the stinkin' thinkin' of past hurts, a sense of over-responsibility, fear of failure or fear of success, past failures and disappointments, shattered dreams, or a hundred other excuses.

Some people don't swing anymore because they're stuck. They swung. They did the marriage counseling and still got divorced. They worked night and day and still did not win the contract. They spent their savings on the best doctors around and still the cancer returned. Swinging does not guarantee success. Baseball teaches us that. Not swinging ensures failure, but sometimes it seems like too much to take one more swing.

As we'll see in chapter twenty-one, a person's bat may be his foe. This is when the instrument that could lead a person to a swing-for-the-fences life is considered or thought to be the thing holding them back. You can control your thoughts. You can decide to swing. For some people, given their life experiences, it might take even more effort than the next person to get the bat off their shoulder and swing. But everyone can control his or her own effort. Less or more—it doesn't matter. All of us can take control of what we put into the game of life. We can decide to live life fully and practice building relationships, exercising diplomacy, listening to a spouse or child, and thinking about how to be part of a work group, and we'll suck less the more we practice. All of life is like one big baseball game where we show up, dig in, and suck less. ❤

In the Batter's Box

There are situations at home, work, and elsewhere in your life that require effort. That effort could be emotional, physical, psychological, or something else. Where are places or situations that require you to control your effort and put forth an "all ya got" kind of effort? How would your relationships change if you controlled your effort and put forth your best? Are there things you'd have to practice first (e.g., new software applications, communication skills, parenting techniques . . .)? What keeps you from taking the bat off your shoulder? What is your bat (indifference, fatigue, hurt, or fear)? This is your bat as foe. Your bat is also your gifts, skills, education, and the things in life that make you successful. What would be different if you let THAT BAT swing at life? This is your bat as friend. In either case, you have to swing.

CHAPTER 8

ALL FOR ONE, ONE FOR ALL:
Value Teamwork

Growing up in a small town in Minnesota had distinct advantages, along with some disadvantages. For one thing, it was not always easy to find enough people to field a team for a game. It was even more difficult to field two teams. We did have some organized leagues with real games when we were older, which lasted a few weeks. Outside of that, however, we had to be pretty creative with how we played baseball. For example, it was common to have an "everlasting pitcher" and an "everlasting catcher." That is, the pitcher and catcher never sat down. They played for both teams. That meant we only needed sixteen players for two teams. The more likely scenario was we just rotated batters and players like a volleyball rotation; everyone just played a very fluid game. If we only had six players or so, we'd play a game called 500, where a person pitched and another one caught while batters rotated through five hits. Players in the field earned points by catching fly balls or scooping up grounders, which then put them into the batter's box.

Interesting, isn't it? All nine players are so integral to the game that without those nine, the game can't be played. Volleyball needs only two people per side. Three-on-three basketball happens all over the place. Nine-man football is common, and even fewer players can keep the game alive. Moreover, the distinctive skills necessary to each position in baseball are obvious. A first baseman needs to be able to stretch like a yoga instructor, keeping his foot on the bag to scoop out a low throw coming in from a fielder. A shortstop has to have range, the ability to shoot side to side quickly, and then to field a bouncing ball cleanly, pivot, and throw to first accurately and hard. Outfielders need to be able to see the ball before they hear it (yes, the sound is late to reach their ears) and have the arm strength to "mail" the ball great distances, right on target, often following long interludes where no ball went past the infield. They have to stay alert and be able to react, even if nothing happens. Third base is called the "hot corner." Not only must the third baseman have quick reactions, but he also has to be able to throw across the diamond on the diagonal, a distance greater than the base path. Pitchers, of course, have to throw a variety of pitches from sixty feet away into a space roughly the size of a breadbox.

All of this is on defense. When it comes to offense, there are players known for their short game. That is, they knock in few home runs but their teammates can generally count on them to get a single or even to bunt runners over from first to second, putting that person into scoring position. Others are known as home run hitters. They often strike out as much as they hit a home run but are obviously necessary to winning games. These people are sometimes designated hitters (in the American League), taking advantage of pitchers not having to bat. There are players known for stealing bases. Getting on base is part of a manager's strategy. The batting order, or when these different hitters appear in the batter's box, mixes short-game people, base stealers, and home run kings, along with people known to crowd the plate (opening themselves to being hit by a pitch) and people who somehow draw a large share of walks.

On offense, as well as defense, every game requires a complete team effort. Although everyone is important, one night will find a player who gets hit after hit, drives in runs, and becomes responsible for four out of the team's five runs. But if the defense doesn't stop runs, the pitcher doesn't strike out batters, double plays aren't turned, and errors aren't avoided, that offensive effort will be for naught. Similarly, games have been won by a score of 1–0. Offense was slight but defense was superb. The players in the field are essential, even if they happen to be good hitters. Key to baseball and one of the hallmarks of the game that I so love is the truism, "I matter because we matter." Tonight, it's you who carried the team with offense. Tomorrow, it's another person's spectacular catch of a ball traveling over the fence that will steal the game-winning run from the opposing batter. We chatter. We support one another. We never give up on us, the team. This is what is meant by "one for all, and all for one."

"It takes a village to raise a child," the saying goes. Anyone who has ever had children knows how absolutely essential it is to have support, in ways both small and great. Working on a national retail rollout of a new product promotion reveals how integral marketing, operations, logistics, sales, and field personnel are to eventual success. Stores can't sell what they can't put on the shelves. There's no point in creating a marketing plan if the field can't execute it or doesn't understand the promotion. And, of course, few people will buy something they have never heard of or seen. Teamwork is relatively obvious in these situations. How does someone value teamwork in everyday situations?

The fabric of our lives is woven with more threads than we might realize at first glance. "No man is an island," wrote John Donne. It's true. We are connected and interconnected in countless ways to people nearby and far away. When I open the door to our office in the morning, I am reminded of the cleaning staff who comes in the middle of the night and makes it possible for us to greet clients. They are part of the team. The security guard greets me so positively that I'm genuinely glad to be there in the morning. She's part of the team. Coffee grown in sustainable fields with sales that support whole villages adds a welcome fragrance to the office as it begins to brew. Those farmers are part of the team. Examples could multiply. The point is, we count on many people, and they count on us, to create and maintain daily life. To value teamwork is to be aware of connectedness, appreciating that all kinds of people make possible the lives we live. And many more people are a part of that life than we might first imagine. The game of life, like the game of baseball, requires the whole team showing up, digging in, and swinging for the fences. We are all in this together and are responsible for one another. A healthy team mindset can help quiet the voices of shame rattling in our heads. ♥

In the Batter's Box

Consider the vast array of people who could be counted among the members of your daily team. Are there ways that you could practice Little League affirmation with them? What are your responsibilities toward them? Now think of disturbing elements, people at war, and societies in distress. If you could create a team mentality (one for all, all for one), what would you do or say differently? How do you or could you value those team members?

CHAPTER 9

IT'S ALL ABOUT FAIRNESS:
Tolerate Unevenness

Most kids, it seems to me, are totally self-centered. It's as if they are the center of the universe. Part of this seems related to basic survival, I would guess. Just like baby birds, the chirping and squawking carried out by infants ensures that older people notice them, attend to their needs, and generally guarantee that they will make it into next week. Based on all the time, money, and effort we expend on those little creatures, they are, in a way, the centers of our universe. Though the chirping and squawking tends to level off as the baby ages, it never seems to go away completely. Even as adults, that sense of self-importance is closer to the surface of some people's skin than others. Part of this squawking is good and keeps us from getting taken advantage of, providing healthy boundaries. Yet, a sense of entitlement is more developed in some people, causing a hypersensitive radar to injustice and a cry of "not fair" when something does not go completely in that person's favor. This is never more true than at bat.

Thankfully, balls and strikes are still called by real, live human umpires. True, they have spent thousands of hours hunched over hundreds of catchers and have seen thousands of pitches. The number of people who attempt to umpire in the Major League far surpasses the few available spots. Nevertheless, those human umpires are subject to the vagaries of weather, playing conditions, and travel that the players and coaches experience. Which is to say, they have good days and bad days. Strike zones can be a little wider or narrower, taller or shorter, on any given day. Pitchers accept this. They learn to tolerate unevenness. What they don't like is inconsistency—wide, narrow, tall, and short—all in the same game. Whatever it is, a consistent strike zone is one piece in making the game as fair as it can be. People, still being people, can see a particular pitch going in their favor when the umpire called it the other way. This is where a swing-for-the-fences mentality that absorbs the lessons of baseball can help, especially learning to tolerate unevenness.

Some calls are simply wrong. Bad. The umpire blew it. If you are the kind of player whose sense of entitlement is acute, you react to unjust situations quickly and fiercely, or if you cannot tolerate unevenness, then bad calls can really rock your world. You lose focus. You begin to swing wildly at pitches. Soon, you are completely ineffective at hitting because you keep returning to the location of every past pitch rather than paying attention to the next one. Since you have never really overcome your sense of being the center of the universe, you cry "not fair" when it's strike three and you have to trudge back to the dugout. Often, you can carry that sense of being wronged into the outfield where you can't focus on your job. You may end up causing errors where winning runs are scored.

Another term for this sense of entitlement that causes hair-trigger responses of outrage at the least whiff of injustice is victimization. People who see themselves as victims and the world as against them at every turn cannot tolerate unevenness. I'm not talking about true victims of hunger, fear, injustice, or oppression. These individuals obviously live in an unfair world. I mean the people who never really grew beyond the chirping and squawking of infancy. They never learned that life is not always fair. They never learned to accept the fact that sometimes people make mistakes and stuff just happens. Always focusing on how they have been slighted or offended, they walk around with chips on their shoulders and criticism spewing from their mouths. A swing-for-the-fences mentality could be helpful in countering that malaise.

Not every call goes your way. There is an unevenness in the game of baseball—it's slight, but not entirely absent. You could say that it's partly a matter of perspective. The umpire saw it one way and made a decision that went against how you saw it, deciding a different way. Fans may agree or disagree, based on allegiances. Tolerating unevenness is such a part of baseball that it's easy to expand its importance.

Go to a Major League game today and witness the wide diversity of players and fans. When Jackie Robinson became the first African-American ballplayer in the Major League, there was such an uproar that his mere presence could spark fights in the park. However, baseball has made great strides in bridging racial and cultural divides. If businesses and organizations wanted to demonstrate cultural diversity and increase sensitivity to the rich variety of people in our country, they could immerse their employees in baseball. Every player has to show up to the game every day, controlling his attitude and his effort. The team has to be a team, constantly uplifting and encouraging one another. They must dig in, focusing on the here and now. They drive for the long haul, never giving up hope or giving in to despair. Failure is a part of our common humanity, making it possible to practice grace toward one another. The meaning-making of baseball is apparent as fans make sense of their world. We can learn a great deal from baseball. It's no wonder it's been such an enduring part of our culture and history. ♥

In the Batter's Box

When things don't go your way at work or home, how do you react? Is that reaction a true reflection of how you feel or do you temper your feelings and react differently? How flexible are you in the face of unevenness in your daily activity? If everything does not run smoothly or according to your plans, what do you feel, think, say, and do? How could going to a baseball game help you increase your awareness of and appreciation for cultural diversity in our world?

CHAPTER 10

ON THE FIELD OF PLAY, EVERYWHERE:
Apply Lessons

Foul poles stand at the corners of every right field and left field in every ballpark around the world. They can be fancy or not. Sometimes, they're just a rock or a stick like the ones we used on our little neighborhood field. The poles mark the edges of official play, the boundaries of regular activity. Everything inside those boundaries is considered "fair" and outside is "foul." They are a part of the lines extending from home plate all along the length of the ballpark's playing surface. A cool thing about those poles is that they only mark the edges of play, not the terminus. That is, the lines that determine fair or foul can be said to go on forever. In a very real sense, therefore, lines of play crisscross the entire earth. Like the invisible lines of latitude and longitude marking our location on a globe, the field of play that is integral to the game of baseball is literally everywhere we happen to be standing. We are on the field of play, everywhere. As we develop our swing-for-the-fences mentality, we can more easily apply the multitude of life lessons we glean from baseball. Hopefully, we'll also be able to counter much of our stinkin' thinkin' that keeps us from realizing our full potential.

The vast majority of any park's playing surface is fair ground, giving every player equal access to a huge opportunity to hit the ball safely and get on base. It's not like a little, tiny net that someone has to throw something into or whack something into. Sure, a baseball field of play is bounded on one end by a large-arched fence, but getting the ball over it just means the batter gets to come home and is said to have scored a run. The lines from home plate, illustrated by the foul poles, mark the field. But even here, there is excess ground. The ball is still in play as it crosses the lines, giving the defense an edge in being able to make outs as they catch fly balls in that territory. But the lines also give batters an edge, as they're able to hit as many foul balls as they like without making an out. The first two are strikes, but after that, it doesn't matter.

The only set dimensions of a ballpark are those of the infield. They are meticulous. It's ninety feet from base to base. From the front edge of the pitcher's rubber, located at the top of the mound, to the apex of home plate is sixty feet and six inches, which is itself a pentagonal shape cut from a seventeen by seventeen-inch square. The pitcher's rubber measures twenty-four inches by six inches. The mound has a radius of nine feet and is ten inches above the surface of home plate. The boxes for catchers, coaches, and batters are clearly marked, measured, and precisely located. Ninety-five feet from the center of the pitcher's mound locates the leading edge of the outfield grass. And on it goes, with the size and placement of on-deck batter's circles, the minimum space from home plate's apex to the backstop, where to end the infield grass and begin the dirt portion of the infield, and so on. Although there are minimums in terms of distance from home plate to either corner of the outfield, there is no maximum (except for obvious restrictions imposed by streets or other physical boundaries of the park's location). Boston's Fenway Park added the famous "Green Monster" in left field, a high wall of thirty-seven feet and two inches, because it's only 310 feet from home plate. Aside from thwarting right-handed hitters, this wall adds an extra dimension to playing left field and high-priced seats for fans who sit on top of it!

The consistency of the infield allows for reliability in playing ball in one park versus another. A double-play ball will require covering the same area and exercising the same maneuverability between shortstop and second base no matter where such play occurs. I look at this as a metaphor for how we all succeed in life. In the parts that matter, how runs are scored and games won, we all have the same chance. Based on our attitude and effort, we can navigate that space more or less successfully than our opponents. This isn't a perfect analogy of course, because not everyone in our society really has the same chances at life that everyone else does. But for the most part, it's a good place to start. Even if someone has been dealt a raw hand, there are ways to move beyond that circumstance. Here, as much as anywhere, a team with a Little League attitude is most critically important.

Outfields vary widely in shape, area covered, and distances between locations. Heights of fences vary widely. This variety could be explained by the fact that in the early days of baseball, the only focus was on creating a consistent infield of play. There were no fences, except those created by the fans standing in an arch beyond the players to watch the games. The fact that outfields are not consistent beyond the minimum distances required is emblematic to me of how much variety there is in the ability to realize one's dreams. If swinging for the fences means that every once in a while my efforts actually pay off, and I realize one of my passions, see a dream come true, or accomplish some significant goal, then actually being able to *do that* requires an environment where those payoffs are possible. Buying a house while saddled with huge student loan debt and a poor-paying job is like hitting in Petco Park when there's a strong wind coming in from center field. This may not be impossible, but it is very difficult.

I come back to the hitters in the ballpark. If I have two strikes on me already, but keep hitting one foul ball after another, I am said to "remain alive" in the count. As long as I keep swinging and getting a piece of the ball, I still have a chance. Think of all those times at work or within a relationship where you had the genesis of an idea, but the project or the relationship just seemed to stay flat. There was no progress visible on any front. You kept swinging, getting little bits of ideas right and little strands of interaction felt right, time after time. You adjusted your stance, so to speak, and opened up to new ideas. No one called you "out" after seventeen attempts. They let you play on until, all of a sudden, there was a breakthrough! You connected on an idea, recognized an endearing quality in the other person, and everything seemed to advance in a positive direction. ❦

In the Batter's Box

In what ways is it true that everyone has the same chances in life to realize their dreams? In what ways is it not true? Is there anything we could do, thinking like a baseball team, to open opportunities for everyone to come closer to realizing their dreams? Describe that picture—what we do, what we sound like, how we create attitudes and encourage effort, ways to counter stinkin' thinkin,' and anything else that could make those dreams a reality.

CHAPTER 11

SEVENTH-INNING STRETCH:
Refresh Regularly

Halftime. Go to any football game, for example, and there will be a set amount of time between two equal halves of play. There will be marching bands, dance lines, cheerleaders, and more. Such a time exists at basketball games. Again, bands play, cheerleaders jump and shout, and dance lines perform. Perhaps a fan could win a new car by throwing a ball from center court into the basket. There are equal breaks between periods at a hockey game. Baseball is different.

Although there is some debate about the actual origin of the seventh-inning stretch, there does seem to be a consensus that it began in the late 1800s. It seems really odd to me that it occurs after the first half of the seventh inning, before the home team comes up to bat. Why not the middle of the fourth inning, halfway through a nine-inning game? Like several things about baseball (such as a pitch count that includes an unequal amount of four balls and three strikes), the seventh-inning stretch is one of those elements of the game that "just is." Some writers contend that it came into being when teams started warming up a relief pitcher for the final two innings. The practical application today is that most vendors stop serving alcohol after the last out of the seventh inning. The short break therefore allows fans to get another cool one before the end of the game.

There are no marching bands, however. For almost a century, fans have stood, stretched, and sung a song. Actually, it's the chorus of a song, written by a guy who had never been to a baseball game before penning the lyrics. Fans sing about going to a game, having snacks, and being more concerned about their team losing than about ever getting back home again. Once at the park, let's just stay there!

Taking time out, creating a break in the action, gives the players a chance to stretch as well. Sitting on a bench, even one that's padded, makes a body stiff after a while. That's why so many players frequently stand in the dugout. A few extra minutes near the end of the game are a welcome relief. Today's modern game also requires exercising strategies and players effectively. Relief pitchers and "closers" earn high salaries for throwing few pitches, but generating outs, which often lead to victories. Deciding to insert a new hitter or to replace a tired outfielder can have consequences also, offensively or defensively. The point is, even during a rest period, something is happening.

Resting is as important as doing. Both are necessary to health and well-being. A car engine that never stops running would soon fall apart or burn up. A man who once worked so much that his family relationships began to suffer was told that even God took a day off, so who did he think he was that he could never take time to relax? Part of his problem was that he literally did not know how to relax or what relaxation even looked like. I have also known people who obsess so much over a relationship or some slight they have experienced that they simply need to short-circuit their thoughts for a few minutes in order to regain their balance.

Sleep is an essential part of our health on a number of levels. As we sleep, soft tissue is repaired, stiff joints loosen up, and toxins are gathered up and readied for disposal. Even our brains are put into a state where we can begin to unlock ideas or solve thorny issues. Our bodies' natural rhythms are reset, and everything from brain function to digestion is put back on track. We've all heard this before, along with how to get the most from our sleep time, such as winding down before bed and not drinking alcohol right before bedtime or watching a scary movie right before sleeping. But what about regular periods of refreshment?

Much research has been done to show the importance of short, regular breaks during the workday. These breaks improve morale as well as productivity. Most Americans don't take all of their skimpy vacations, let alone the four or five weeks common across Europe, much to their detriment. Those vacations, however, are opportunities to unhook from the daily grind. As if stopping the car engine for a while, that person has a chance to relax her heart, steady breathing, regulate digestion, focus on new thoughts, and avoid burning out overall.

The practices of yoga, journaling, meditation, reading sacred literature, and even being still before diving into the evening meal are all ways of regularly refreshing oneself. Viewed separately, these activities may seem inconsequential (like a short seventh-inning stretch). Over a period of a lifetime, however, they become part of the rhythm of one's life. Oceans ebb and flow. Trees and plants grow, sprout, and rest. Seasons change.

The beauty of baseball is that even though stretching, taking a short pause before the end of the game, is hardly symmetrical (and therefore not "perfect"), doing so game after game, year after year, creates consistency. It's a regular, predictable moment of refreshment. Practiced over the long-haul season of one's life, it creates a sense of renewal. Refreshing yourself with daily moments of renewal will keep you from burning up, losing your edge, or destroying your important relationships. Here, too, you have to show up, dig in, and suck less. You don't have to be perfect in your yoga poses or expert at putting your thoughts into a notebook. It's up to you to control your attitude and effort. Decide to enter into a rhythm of refreshment. You'll never want to go back to a place of constant, driving effort where the end result is burnout and destruction. Let baseball help you. ♥

In the Batter's Box

If you have a regular routine of exercise, meditation, journaling, prayer, and so on, reflect for the next two weeks on how those moments of refreshment make a difference in your life. If you do not have such a routine, consider adding one element of regular refreshment to your daily life. Perhaps it's as simple as everyone pausing for a moment at the evening meal before scarfing up the food. You could add one more moment of refreshment in another month, if you desire. Maybe you want to take the next two weeks to take a short snack break before the end of the day. Taking a few minutes to think about what you're doing is a swing-for-the-fences mentality that's been in effect for generations. It's what keeps the game of baseball alive and well—and it could do the same for you.

CHAPTER 12

EVERYONE CAN
TEACH EVERYONE:
Be Coachable

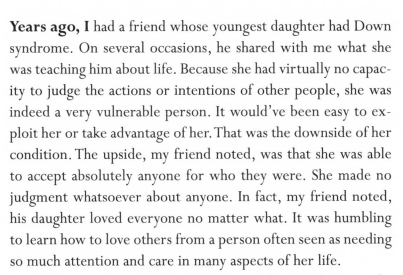

Years ago, I had a friend whose youngest daughter had Down syndrome. On several occasions, he shared with me what she was teaching him about life. Because she had virtually no capacity to judge the actions or intentions of other people, she was indeed a very vulnerable person. It would've been easy to exploit her or take advantage of her. That was the downside of her condition. The upside, my friend noted, was that she was able to accept absolutely anyone for who they were. She made no judgment whatsoever about anyone. In fact, my friend noted, his daughter loved everyone no matter what. It was humbling to learn how to love others from a person often seen as needing so much attention and care in many aspects of her life.

Major League teams have hitting coaches, pitching coaches, fielding coaches, and even bench coaches. Seriously! A bench coach works with players sitting by to jump into the game either for offense or defense and to keep up their affirming chatter. Keeping everyone "in" the game is a key component of the bench coach's job. They also serve as the manager should the main guy be ejected from the game. Hitting coaches may have had some success in their playing careers but are valued for what they are able to teach others: how to approach certain pitchers, adjustments that may help when digging into the batter's box, and mental exercises that help batters out of hitting slumps. Everyone can teach everyone something. We learn and grow from our interactions with others.

We've got a name for someone who is a self-absorbed, narcissistic, and arrogant person whom others avoid or talk about disparagingly: a know-it-all. Such a person is unteachable and drags down the morale of the team. Unable to accept coaching, that person goes through life without the richness, insight, or "aha" moments made possible by opening up to others. People who view themselves as superstars, better than everyone else, often strut about oblivious to others, and expect everyone to be in awe of them or even cater to their every whim—hardly the characteristics that make for a solid, winning team.

A know-it-all is not open to coaching. Such openness requires the person to be vulnerable, not like my friend's daughter (in the sense of truly exploitable), but open to criticism and critique. Such a person will understand that he or she does not have everything together, as we say, and is not perfect in every way. Baseball, remember, counts three times out of ten as being good enough. The kind of openness necessary for productive coaching means that someone is willing to be vulnerable (in the sense of having a willingness to be seen as weak or even deficient in some areas), which is the very opposite of a know-it-all. A coachable person knows that he is not hitting the ball as effectively as he could and wants help knowing how to adjust his hips or what to do with his wrists. Admitting that he needs help is a sign of strength, an indication that he wants to get better and is willing to put himself out there and let someone else guide him. There is always the risk that someone could make fun of him. In baseball, however, coaches and players alike would meet that kind of jeering from a teammate with swift retribution.

From the earliest days in a player's career, all the way back to Little League, one is constantly learning the lesson of being coachable. Spring training reinforces lessons learned as a kid. Fundamentals (throwing, fielding, hitting, and running) are practiced ad infinitum, daily, and throughout the long-haul season. If you are not coachable, you simply cannot play baseball. There is another phenomenon that happens between people who are coachable and open to learning and self-improvement. This vulnerability actually makes individuals and relationships stronger. There is truth to the statement "we are made strong in our weakness." You know this if you have ever shared a personal fear, shortcoming, or broken heart with someone close to you. That person's acceptance of you, and perhaps sharing with you in return, puts you in the same boat. You've both had that same kind of hurt, disappointment, or failure in your life but have persevered. After such sharing, there is a quiet understanding of what each has been through in life. There's an appreciation of each other. It's hard to turn your backs on each other, and it's easier to let some things slide, such as the annoying way they chew their toast.

Baseball players understand this. Being coachable means that everyone is working to get as good as they can get for the sake of the team. Each player in turn is counting on all the others. No one is perfect. No one "has it all together." Everyone can learn something, and in fact, needs to improve to the best of his ability for the team to advance. Through the years, I have encountered people who have played baseball and have had extensive experience being coachable. I find that they do really well on work teams, learning product specifications, trying new approaches, and generally building solid relationships with coworkers. Perhaps I've been fortunate to meet the exceptional players, but I doubt it. For the most part, I'd want someone with a swing-for-the-fences mentality working with me any day. ❦

In the Batter's Box

There is a risk involved in being open and sharing one's vulnerability or weakness with another person. With whom in your life could you risk such openness? Identify such a person and share a fear, shortcoming, or some brokenness that has left you deficient in a part of your life that you want strengthened (e.g., perhaps you have difficulty trusting others because of a past relationship). Notice what happens as you open up with each other. What possibilities await you as you strengthen your ability to be coachable?

CHAPTER 13

DON'T TAKE IT PERSONALLY:
Flush Codependency

"The ump hates me," said one of my teammates, trudging back to the dugout after a called third strike.

"What are you talking about?" asked the coach.

"That's the second time he called a third strike on me," whined the player.

"Then next time you're down two strikes, you better swing," continued the coach. "That way, you might hit the ball."

Tough words for a twelve-year-old kid to hear, or so I thought at the time. Looking back on it through the years, I realize that the coach was right. The kid needed to swing. We all need to swing. There's no guarantee that we'll connect and be successful. There is, however, a guarantee that we'll fail should we just stay put. It's not that some umpire or arbitrary situation has our number and is out to get us. That kind of thinking illustrates that the person's belief system puts them at the center of the universe. Well, for anyone reading this, you know by now that not one of us is the center of the universe. If you find yourself whining about some personal injustice, like a called third strike, or "always" getting in the wrong line at the grocery store, it is not because some force in the universe is picking on you.

The psychological term for that kind of thinking (that stinkin' thinkin') is external locus of control. We see life and situations happening *to us* outside of our personal control or effort. Helpless against the raging tide of life, we are tossed to and fro. With such a mindset, one is often subject to the whims of other people. Feeling weak but not sharing such vulnerability with a trusted other, such a person gets clues about how to act (or even think) from someone else or from the situation itself. I saw this a lot when working with teenagers as a parish priest. Too many kids got their sense of self-worth by being a part of the "in crowd." The cool kids may have been acting in destructive or inappropriate ways but being part of that group was, in some teens' mind, far better than being outside of it.

Codependency is another term. I'm okay if you're okay, even if that means I constantly compromise personal values or beliefs in order to be with you. Unless you love me, I am worthless. I'm still giving up control of my thoughts and actions in order to satisfy you. We are not a team of coequal partners. It's one up (you) and one down (me). Oddly enough, allowing myself to stay in such a relationship does not require me to change. I don't have to be coachable. I don't have to take any responsibility for the success or failure of this relationship. I can play the victim and whine about how everything works against me (the ump always calls a third strike on me) in the game of life.

Enter a swing-for-the-fences mentality. Show up. Dig in. Suck less. Once again, baseball can teach us how to live happier lives. NEWS FLASH: you are not the center of the universe. Don't take it personally if you get a called third strike in life (e.g., pick the wrong line at the grocery store or hit a string of red lights in traffic). No one and no thing is out to get you. Life happens. You cannot expect others to carry you through life. You have to do your part. Swing. That's all we ask. You can't swing if you don't show up. You won't hit unless you control your attitude and effort. No one is looking for perfection. We're looking for a solid baseball player—someone who is coachable, practices, digs in, and is part of the team. Flush the codependent mindset of having someone or something else define you. You're good enough to be on this team. So be on it, be part of it, and do your best. That's all we expect and all we need. ♥

In the Batter's Box

Being part of a baseball team means that everyone has to contribute to the best of their ability. Everyone counts on everyone else. Whining because the umpire called a third strike does not get anyone's sympathy, and it does not move the team forward or win games. Swing the bat. Describe a situation or relationship in which *you* have to swing *your* bat and where *you* need to do *your* part to move forward. How does flushing codependency help (i.e., not seeing yourself as the victim of outside influences)?

CHAPTER 14

A MEANING-MAKING GAME:
Practice Ritual

I love keeping score at a baseball game. There's something about the graphic nature of the game that I love to see laid out before me on the sheets of the scorebook. I like drawing lines of runners as they advance around the bases. I love filling in the diamonds as runs are scored, especially if it's my team. And I like that I journal the events of our family in the margins of the scorebook. You can read the history of our family (or short snippets of it) through the lens of baseball. It's a part of the ritual I enjoy when going to a game, as with getting a grilled meat-like substance and cold brew upon entering the park. I bring order to my chaotic life, at least momentarily, in some small measure, by going to a game and practicing all my little rituals in the process.

Rituals. Goodness knows, baseball has them! I can write about the ones that come to mind, you will add some, and yet even more will be discovered down the road. A game that is America's favorite pastime simply cannot survive for well over a century without rituals. Rituals provide meaning, structure, and an understanding of life and our role in it. We are not just here to provide carbon dioxide for the weeds. Rituals can help alleviate our grief, reduce our anxiety before stressful tasks, and increase our confidence in facing difficult situations.

Wade Boggs, the former third baseman for the Boston Red Sox, had some interesting rituals. He got up every day at exactly the same time. He ate chicken before every game. He did his batting practice at 5:15, took 117 ground balls, and then ran sprints at exactly 7:17 before each game (whenever it was an evening game, that is). It's reported that he would write the Hebrew word for "living" in the dirt before stepping up to the plate. He was not Jewish. Did all of this work? For him, it did. He was inducted into the Baseball Hall of Fame in 2005. He had over 3,000 hits in his career, with a .328 batting average. His .415 on-base percentage meant that in over 2,400 games, he reached base successfully in 80 percent of them. In 1985, he had the highest batting average the Red Sox had seen since Ted Williams, nearly thirty years earlier, and his 240 hits were the most in over fifty years. He may have been born to hit baseballs like some kids were born to play piano, as his mother reportedly said, but his rituals focused him on his task, calmed his nerves, provided the structure he needed, and gave him the confidence to do what he needed to do.

There are many rituals that are not so unique as Mr. Boggs' rituals. Nevertheless, they help us overcome anxiety before a difficult task, calm our nerves in the midst of a stressful situation, orient our focus in the face of competing claims, and otherwise give us a sense of control in life. This is evident in religious observances around birth, death, and marriage, for example. Family gatherings around holidays are replete with rituals (why do we eat that only now?). Without ritual, we simply bounce from one thing to another in life. Even a morning shower helps orient ourselves, our thoughts, and our feelings to another new day. Rituals are mindless, in the sense of being so natural that we do not consciously think about them. We brush and floss our teeth before bedtime. We have family night on the couch every Sunday, with popcorn and a movie, unless something really big causes us not to, and then we deal with the disruption to our lives by gathering for ice cream after that event.

During times of war, from fighting with each other during the Civil War to fighting countries around the world, we have played baseball. When cities have been torn apart by racial and social divides, we have played baseball. When we have faced terrible political or economic challenges, we have played baseball. Times of natural disaster or terrorist attacks have not kept us from playing baseball. Refusing to let chaos reign, bringing some measure of sanity and control back to our lives, we have turned to baseball to calm our troubled souls. Baseball has brought us together in ways that nothing else could. There is something special about a country swinging for the fences. We show up. Dig into the tasks at hand. Suck less. We never get it quite right. We're never perfect. But we're there, together. All our crazy rituals (wearing special shirts, filling out score sheets, drawing marks in the dirt, readjusting batting gloves after every pitch, and tapping our bats with chicken bones) come together to create meaning for us. We are, in some small measure, in control of our lives or at least responsible for them, even if it doesn't seem like it at the moment. So, we've got this. We're okay. Batter up! Play ball! ♥

In the Batter's Box

If you're feeling out of control and swept up by the whirlwind of life, put some "mindless" (i.e., non-conscious) ritual into your day. Practice getting up at a set time. Spend some time in reflection, prayer, meditation, or sacred reading. What about that morning walk? Get into a habit of some kind that takes the same shape every day, and do it for the next month. Put your feelings down now and compare them to your feelings that you express a month from now. Did your feelings change? What role did ritual play in the change?

CHAPTER 15

IT'S ALL IN THE MOMENT:
Focus Diligently

Half a second. That's about how much time it takes for a baseball to reach the batter after leaving the pitcher's hand. Approximately sixty feet away, the ball is traveling close to a hundred miles an hour, a little less as it crosses home plate or meets the bat. The batter has to decide to swing and then actually do it if something is to happen. The batter is usually ready in his stance, with bat up, eyes trained on the mound, and weight on his back foot. Then, as the ball makes its journey, he twists his hips, extends his arms as he swings the bat, rolls his wrists, and follows through. He hits the ball or not. Oh, and he has a split second to gauge whether or not the ball will be a strike (and something he should hit) or be called a ball (and a pitch to avoid). The reader may be stymied by seeing a batter twisted in knots by a pitch, swinging way ahead of the ball or chasing something that was so *obviously* outside or in the dirt. Pitchers today have ways of holding the ball and throwing it in a manner that curves, dives, and appears to float toward home plate. It's just not as simple as hitting the whiffle ball that your dad tossed you in the driveway as a kid.

Focus. It is *that moment* when the batter commits to swinging at the ball which can determine what comes next. It could be the game-winning home run or the last out of the last game of the season. A savvy pitcher will throw a mix of pitches to a hitter in order to confuse him. A series of high, inside fastballs can get a hitter to sit back a little. Then, throwing curve balls low and outside can make the batter reach for something less than perfect, only to be closed with a "changeup" (a pitch that is delivered with the same arm and body motions as a fastball but held in such a way that it travels much slower to the plate), causing the batter to swing too early and miss. Hitters cannot get lazy and assume one pitch or another will come their way. Knowing the pitcher's style helps. But the batter must renew his focus after every single pitch in order to stay alive at the plate. A bad call by the umpire can certainly be upsetting, but the batter must shrug it off if he is to remain focused.

Players in the field must turn their attention to every pitch and rehearse in their minds what they're going to do should the ball come their way, perhaps a hundred times every game or even more, should the game go extra innings. Catchers not only do that, but they call every pitch, 162 games during the regular season. Add a dozen more games if they go on to the World Series. Getting caught up in what's coming next week or even tomorrow is the job of coaches and managers. Players focus on the here and now. Likewise, dwelling on what did or did not happen last week or even yesterday is a waste of time. Again, it will be the job of coaches and managers to develop drill plans to address anything that's needed. Such singularity of focus makes it virtually impossible to keep ragging on someone's errant throw in a game two days ago that led to the go-ahead run. Focus. Do the job your teammates expect from you. And move on. Together.

Keeping a scorebook helps a fan focus. It is very easy to wander mentally while sitting at a ball game. A lot of people do it. Just listen to the buzz of the crowd talking and laughing. It seems, however, that scoring is going out of fashion, maybe because many people at a game simply cannot focus that diligently for that long. I can tell you from experience that whatever else may be crying out for attention from your brain cells (work, school, kids, relationships, obsessive thoughts, or troubles), you do not have time or the ability to do anything else but focus on the game while you're immersed in scoring. It's magic how after intensely focusing on a game for a couple of hours of scoring, I feel energized, refreshed, and clear-headed. Maybe it's just me, but I don't think I'm that unique.

As a therapist working with people who live in chemically-dependent family systems, I noticed how people can think about and dwell on certain issues, people, or disappointments over and over again. At times, it is almost useless to point out alternatives because their thoughts and memories are so reflexively trained to think only one way. Replaying the same story of hurt suffered and rude behavior of a spouse at a dinner party may have enabled the other spouse to feel self-righteous playing the injured martyr and might have resulted in soothing words from a friend. But after a while, such victimhood would wear thin, and the friend would move on to more productive relationships. This self-absorbed focus is not the liberating focus of baseball. It's unhealthy and destroys the chances of real intimacy with another person. It is not the focus of the here and now. It's part of the stinkin' thinkin' of there and then.

Baseball can teach us how to set ourselves up for healthier living. Using batters swinging for the fences as our guide, we can focus diligently on the here and now. We can control our attitudes, decide to show up, and dig in. We can control our efforts and suck less. Success might attend our efforts and that's great, but tomorrow will be another day. Failure will not be the final word, either. That we get it right three times out of ten will matter and be good enough. Focus. ♥

In the Batter's Box

Name two things that constantly spin around in your thoughts, annoying you like crazy. Write them down and put that piece of paper aside (you can always come back to those annoying thoughts later if you want). Now, listen to or watch one complete inning of baseball while keeping score (see chapter twenty-seven). How does that feel? Have your annoying thoughts dissipated or disappeared altogether? Try another couple of innings, as needed.

CHAPTER 16

WHEN STEALING MAKES SENSE:
Take Risks

Once again, because of the way stolen bases were calculated and since "caught stealing" statistics were not all that reliable until the twentieth century, talking about who is the greatest base stealer of all time is a bit fuzzy. For our purposes, however, we're going with Rickey Henderson. Rickey Henderson of the Oakland Athletics (the A's) holds the Major League record of 1,406 career-stolen bases. Lou Brock, who would arguably come in second place, has 468 less at 938. Rickey was still going strong when, at age thirty-nine, he became the oldest player in Major League history to lead the Bigs in steals. He had sixty-six steals that year. His lifetime average is fifty-six steals per season with an astonishing 81 percent success rate (rounded up). Only two men since 1900 have stolen 100 or more bases in three separate seasons: Rickey Henderson and Vince Coleman. That's a successful steal two out of every three games.

Being able to get on base, meaning first base, and subsequently steal second, is a part of some teams' offensive strategy. Perhaps the team does not have many players who can hit long balls (i.e., home runs), so it must rely on manufacturing runs with "small ball" tactics. A runner on second base can generally score from there, even if the batter only hits a single. Having Rickey Henderson in the lead-off position (i.e., batting first in the lineup) with his ability to get to second was very effective for the Oakland A's back in the 1980s. Reading the pitcher is key. The best base stealers notice small actions of the opposing pitcher. They can tell if he intends to throw over to first or complete the pitch. It could be that the pitcher digs his toe into the dirt next to the rubber, getting set to push off his leg for the throw to home, thus signaling to the would-be base stealer that he might have a chance to take second. The poor catcher then has to concentrate on catching the ball (provided the batter doesn't hit it) and throw down to second base with the hope that his teammate tags out the runner. Usually, the runner gets there first. Stealing third base or even home is not as common, although when it happens successfully it is truly exciting.

It's always risky to steal. If the runner takes off for the next base and the hitter pops up, he could be caught in a double play. That is, a fielder could catch the pop-up and throw to the base from which the runner just launched, resulting in two outs (the runner would have to get back to the base in order to "tag up" before advancing). A runner intending to steal could stand too far away from the base and not be able to get back in time before the pitcher throws over, thus getting tagged out. The base stealer could inadvertently distract his teammate at the plate and cause him to lose concentration and somehow spoil his at bat. There are no guarantees that the runner will arrive safely, not get injured, or eventually score. His actions could cost his team the lead or even the game. It could also mean a win. That's the way it is with risks. They work or they don't. If you have Little League affirmation and support at your back, taking risks is easier to do than if you know you'll be constantly shamed for blowing it, should the risk not succeed.

Stinkin' thinkin' enters the scene. Too afraid of harping voices should things not turn out, people often stop short of changing course, stepping out, and taking the risk that might forever improve their lives. It must be noted here that I am not talking about doing something stupid or clearly ill-advised, such as jumping onto a subway track or driving fast on a snow-covered mountain road. It's more like musicians who have practiced long and hard who finally take a leap of faith by moving to an area where they can play with others who will challenge, stretch, and teach, making them even better. Rickey Henderson repeatedly practiced sprinting toward second base, perfecting his jump, his run, and his slide with others who constantly challenged him to get better.

Taking risks is scary. They don't always work. Knowing one's abilities and having faith in them, looking for subtle timing clues in exercising a risk, and having meaningful support from others are all key factors in taking calculated risks. With risk comes reward. How many of us took a risk getting married when we did and to whom? Have you ever considered having children a risk-free adventure? Who has ever moved across country for a job or to follow a dream? How many of those life-altering events can you look back on and say that you would do the same thing today?

In 2015, my wife and I left our home, jobs, and lifestyle to move to Tennessee in order to form a three-generation household with our daughter and her family. Six of us live under one roof—four adults and two kids, plus a dog and a cat. We live in an area of the country that we had only visited, never imagining that we would ever call this home. Being cold-weather people by nature, the summers in the South are beyond what we would have thought possible for anyone to survive. We have no plan B. Neither do they. We are all committed to discovering what it means to be a three-gen family (as it's fashionably called) in today's world. Risks, calculated risks, and no guarantees abound. The rewards, great and small, and some yet to be revealed, are around us virtually every day. The economic advantages of scale and having four drivers are readily apparent. Other pluses are cumulative, such as snuggles when we watch a movie or long conversations with grown children after the little ones are in bed. By showing up through the long-haul season of life, being fully present and attentive, digging into the tasks at hand, and sucking less through practice, teamwork, and support, this three-gen family is changing all of us (and those who encounter us) in profound and wonderful ways. ♥

In the Batter's Box

What's the riskiest thing you have ever done and how did it turn out? What are one or two risks with which you now wrestle? How are your skills and experiences uniquely suited to realizing success in exercising that risk? What keeps you from "going for it"? What would it feel like to just go for it? What's waiting for you at the other end?

CHAPTER 17

DO SMALL THINGS WELL:
Execute Daily

Do you always make your bed in the morning? I once lived with a guy in college who would buy new sheets at the beginning of each term and throw the old ones away. At night, he'd grab the sheets and his blanket, stand up to wrap them all around himself, and flop onto his bed. He also used to pile up his dirty dishes in the bathtub and soak them all night. Unfortunately, the drain plug did a poor job of holding water, so in the morning there would be slimy dishes and a horrible ring in the tub. I'm not Mr. Neat by any means, but even he stretched my boundaries. It's funny how little things can become big irritations if not addressed. On the other hand, little things done well and executed faithfully can make all the difference in the world.

I read once about a particular batter who was going through a dreadful slump. He had not had a hit in over fifteen games. It was affecting his morale and draining the energy from his teammates. They wanted to support him, but it was becoming more difficult every passing day that he went without a hit, especially since he made multiple times more money than they did. He was on the team primarily for his bat. So he went to work. Taking extra batting practice was only going to reinforce a bad habit. Something he was doing was just off and needed addressing before he got back into the cage. The batting coach noticed that he was a fraction of a second late in twisting his hips. His arms were not extending, and he was not rolling his wrists all the way. Each little element by itself was probably not causing the slump, but together, they added up to poor performance and contributed to a lousy attitude. Doing these small things well and executing them every day would, the coach surmised, change the results for this very talented hitter.

It worked. He soon began to get hit after hit and helped his team win games. His attitude improved. The team's morale and spirits lifted. They seemed to be having fun playing ball once more. He continued to practice these newfound routines over and over again until they became his new habits. Fans and press alike marveled at the player being back (as if he had gone on sabbatical) and how he looked like a new hitter in the box. The fact that he focused on a few little things and practiced them relentlessly certainly did not make as good a story as some dramatic breakthrough in the player's life. That's the way it is with little things. They matter a great deal in the bigger scheme of life but are too often not within our focus. They're easy to miss, as we look for dramatic activities that will create revolutionary changes in our lives, when it could be that that simple little activity is all we really need.

Small things done well and executed daily can have very positive consequences. Our grandchildren are extremely hungry at 4:00 p.m. every day. Although they eat lunch, it is often the case that they do not eat all of what was packed. It's also a long way from a lunch served at 10:45 a.m. to our family meal at 6:00 p.m., which, of course is only a problem during the school year. They get restless, have short tempers, and generally turn into growling alligators. My wife recognized this early in the game and works at being one step ahead of the curve. Having food ready to go and in their mouths before they get too cranky makes a huge difference in our family life! They become calm, reasonable human beings. They can focus on other things besides fighting with each other or being crabby. And then our family mealtime is a pleasant experience! Small things done well and executed daily can have very positive consequences.

Pepper is a game played at all levels of baseball. A batter hits ground balls and line drives to fielders about twenty to twenty-five feet away, using a soft swing. The fielders, in turn, throw the ball back to the batter who then hits another ground-er or line drive. This is good practice for both the fielder and the hitter. Both have to be quick, focused, alert, and "on their feet" so that they can catch or hit accordingly. It develops and strengthens eye-hand coordination. It helps warm up fielders who have to be ready to move side to side during the game. And it serves as a healthy, competitive warm-up for players as they mentally prepare for the game. Little League affirmation, along with good-natured ribbing, attends a pregame routine of pep-per. Executed daily, this small thing helps improve skills as well as maintain camaraderie. During the long-haul season of 162 games, players would have worked hours on these critical skills and had fun in the process. Who knows how this affects any one particular game? Clearly, it's important overall or teams would abandon the practice altogether. ❦

In the Batter's Box

Small things done well and executed daily can have profound effects on our lives and the lives of those around us. Consider one or two small activities that you could execute daily (at work, home, or school) with friends, family, or colleagues. Do it for two weeks or a month. See what happens to the morale, productivity, or functioning of the group. What did you notice? Describe your attitude and the attitude of the group. What do you like about what you see?

CHAPTER 18

EVERYTHING COMES AROUND:
Demonstrate Respect

I had a Little League coach who said that how we treat everyone on the field is a mirror of how we treat everyone "out there" (and he'd point across the street). He meant that baseball has a lot to teach us about how to become good citizens. I didn't really appreciate what he was saying. It sounded a little corny at the time, but I didn't want to laugh. However, there is a great deal of truth in that statement. If taken as an illustration of how best to treat others, baseball is a wonderful opportunity to practice respect, along with a host of other life skills. If used as a description of how we actually treat people, then the statement is still true. Being rude, inconsiderate, disrespectful, acting like the center of the universe, strutting around with chips on our shoulders, and more while on the baseball field may be a good indication of distasteful behavior off the field. Once again, baseball teaches us lessons to make life better every day.

Pitchers take several warm-up tosses from the mound before the game starts. The umpire squats behind the catcher to get a good look at his arm motion and to determine whether or not he can control his pitches and if he and his catcher are in sync. The pitcher gets a sense of where the umpire's strike zone will be and if he'll be consistent with it. So, if it looks like the ump has a wide but thin strike zone, the pitcher will be encouraged to throw low strikes and hope that batters don't "turn" on inside pitches to crank them over the fence. You will often see pitchers and umpires discussing this strike zone just to be clear. It's one way that they demonstrate respect for each other. Likewise, during a game, the catcher may have a foul tip ricochet off his body. The umpire will stop play, walk around, and sweep the plate with his little broom, giving the catcher some breathing room to recover. It's a way of demonstrating respect. Umpires know what it's like behind the plate.

Respect for your teammates is essential. We've seen how teams that practice Little League skills of affirmation and support have more fun, and maybe even win more games, than teams that are always criticizing one another. Around the field, respect for others is critical. The opposition may try to distract the home team batters with catcalls, only to find themselves the subject of taunts by fans while in the field or at bat. Sometimes, rivalry takes on a menacing tension between teams. A pitcher may throw too close to the batter's head. A base runner may try to take out the defender by sliding into him, hoping to cut him with cleats or hurt his leg. The disrespect mounts until something happens, the benches clear, a brawl breaks out, and the umpires eject people. Fan reaction turns ugly. The serenity of baseball is lost and a toxic bloom of anger hangs over the field.

Respect does not mean that we have to tolerate bad behavior. It does not mean that we justify other people's words or actions as okay, when they really aren't, because they come from a different background or culture. It does mean, however, that not everything has to be exactly on our terms. Not all calls are going to go our way. Live with it. Focus on the next pitch. Have a short-term memory. It's not the end of the world if something is not just the way we want it.

Baseball runs on respect. Pitchers respect certain batters and work hard to make it difficult for them to get anything good to hit. Base runners respect the throwing arms of certain outfielders, so they might not try to stretch a single into a double. Teams that respect their fans and appreciate them see ticket sales remain strong. The Chicago Cubs, for example, nearly always have sellout crowds, even when they don't win over ninety games a year, because fans enjoy themselves at Wrigley Field and know that their team appreciates them. Taking a called third strike, standing tall while walking back to the dugout, and not badmouthing the umpire demonstrate respect for the game (even if it was a bad call). Human beings call those balls and strikes. Sometimes, they get it wrong. Move on, it's not the end of the world.

I had interactions with a vocational training school once that was one of the most respectful places I have ever encountered. Students were addressed as "Mister so-and-so," wore ties, and replied with "yes, sir" and "no, sir" to instructors. They knew that there was zero tolerance for being late, having incomplete assignments, or showing disrespect to anyone. Expectations were clarified at the beginning of every school year. When students started getting dismissed because of disrespecting the rules, fellow students, or instructors, others doubled down on their own positive words, interactions, and assignments. This approach created an atmosphere of trust where people were free to fail, learn, get better, and grow as students and especially as good citizens. They were so upbeat and respectful, it was a delight to engage them. I am not surprised that they have a 100 percent placement record for their graduates. ▼

In the Batter's Box

Compare and contrast situations where you experienced respectful interactions among people and those that were not respectful. What were you thinking? How did you feel? How would you describe those situations, especially any outcomes, reflecting on them now? What are you doing now that creates an atmosphere of respect at work, home, school . . . ?

CHAPTER 19

TAKE ONE FOR THE TEAM:
Sacrifice Easily

It was late in the game. There was a runner on first base. The batter was known to be a power hitter but was in a terrible slump, even striking out twice already that night. The coach really wanted to move the runner along but was not sure if his star slugger could deliver. He asked the player to bunt. The runner on first saw the sign by the third-base coach, pulling twice on the bill of his cap, forget all the other slaps and taps. The pitcher dug his toe into the front of the rubber, a clear indication of his intent to throw home. In the blink of an eye, the runner broke for second, the batter turned to face the mound, and a spinning baseball died on the infield grass within reach of the catcher. It had been a successful bunt. The catcher's only play was to first. The batter was out. The runner successfully moved into scoring position. The power hitter went "oh for three" (0–3) that night. He had no hits and no runs batted in—nothing to show for his efforts, or so it seemed. The next batter was the "star" of the game. It was his single to the gap in left-centerfield that allowed the runner to score the winning run. When the local sports reporter asked him about it, the player demonstrated respect for his slumping teammate who had set them up by laying down a perfect bunt. He was gracious in his remarks.

The thing about sacrifices, however, is they often go unnoticed. How many miles did we put on the car driving kids to practice, lessons, and birthday parties? Can anyone count the sleepless nights spent walking a teething baby? Have you ever done what she wanted to do, even though that's not fun for you? Have you ever eaten at that place because it's his favorite, when you'd rather be somewhere else? Although these maybe aren't sacrifices in the same sense as moving a runner into scoring position, we nevertheless have examples in our lives from times when we put our needs or desires aside for the sake of someone else. The greater good required us to think of the whole, not just ourselves, and swing. But someone will notice, and appreciate it, and say something at some point in time. Or not. But we do it anyway.

Sacrifice is one of the most interesting human phenomena I can imagine. Giving up, giving in, relinquishing control, surrendering to *something* or *someone* in order to improve the current situation for everyone is what makes relationships stronger. Community bonds are tightened. Others are touched in profound ways by the sacrifice of others. There are dramatic times when people sacrifice life or limb for others, like during combat. Those events are recounted and honored, as they should be. The daily, small, and unnoticeable sacrifices by friends, teachers, parents, nonprofit workers, and colleagues at work are the acts that keep communities together. The office manager probably won't get a raise, certainly not a medal, but her actions will strengthen the office and make for a more pleasant workspace when she bakes birthday cupcakes the night before and comes in early to celebrate a colleague's special day. I know a guy who hated his job, flipped between day and night shifts, and willed himself out of bed to go to work. If he could only get himself pointed to the bathroom, he reasoned, he'd make it. He told himself to do so, for his wife and kids. And he did it for seven years before things changed.

Counter to the center of the universe mindset, personal sacrifice is decidedly "others focused." However, thinking of the team, the family, and the group over oneself is not necessarily an outward expression of codependency. Codependency, as we discussed earlier, sees those sacrificing people diminished in stature, strength, or esteem. It would be obvious that they think so little of themselves that making another person happy is the only thing that matters—not the health of the larger whole. In fact, they could fall into the role of a martyr, milking their sacrifice for personal gain. True sacrifice is where the individual remains strong, even in his or her apparent weakness (like being thrown out at first base), because the person has advanced the cause of the team. It would be easy to sacrifice for others when you know that they noticed it, appreciated it, and rewarded you for it. That's why Little League affirmation is so important. It keeps people going, creating conditions where people can sacrifice for the team.

What if sacrificing for the sake of the team is simply the right thing to do, but no one noticed or said anything? Kids are probably never really going to understand, appreciate, or say anything about parents getting them to practice on time after a tough day at the office. In their minds, that's just what parents do. To the extent that personal reward is involved at all, seeing them have fun, learn important life lessons, and get healthy exercise could be all that a parent gets in return. That's enough. So, we keep sacrificing.

Putting aside oneself, personal desires, wishes, and preferences is not necessarily a job description, even though we do a lot of that as parents. There certainly are aspects of every job that people dislike. I'm not sure what difference it would make if we did them poorly or not at all. Poor performance on the undesirable aspects of our jobs might make our business group less productive, but would our workspaces be less fun or our relationships weaker? Yet, sacrificing, especially doing so effortlessly, does make a difference in families, marriages, and at work when it's done for the sake of strengthening the larger whole. That's why "taking one for the team" is such a strong statement. As individuals, and collectively, we are better off because of other people's sacrifices. Likewise, we strengthen the group because of our sacrifices. We show up. We dig in. We suck less as we swing for the fences in all our manifold relationships. ❧

In the Batter's Box

"Sacrifice" and "being a martyr" are not the same. How would you describe the difference? Where can you "take one for the team," and what difference would it make? Think about a situation where someone made a sacrifice for you and thereby strengthened relationships around you. Describe how you felt and the difference it made for the larger group.

CHAPTER 20

EVERYONE BLOWS IT:
Forgive Generously

Sacrifice is putting aside oneself for the good of the whole and for the strength of relationships. As difficult as that action is, forgiving another person is even harder. If sacrifice is something we do for others, forgiveness is what we do for ourselves. Usually, offending actions or words take place prior to the need for forgiveness. There might even be the presence of trauma or victimization. The forgiving person does not say, by way of forgiveness, that everything is okay, we can forget about the offense, let's move forward. The forgiver does not relinquish the right to restitution in some fashion. What is critical to forgiveness is not what we do or say to another person for his or her sake. It's what we do or say that makes us feel better. Especially letting go of anger, which, as we all know, is toxic to our health and well-being.

Playing 162 games a year, often in very hot and humid weather, can put people on edge. Long road trips, sleeping in different hotels, eating in restaurants, and playing in different ballparks every four days can wear thin the patience of people who are often very easygoing. Even players at lower levels get frustrated with teammates who don't hustle after fly balls, aren't swinging the bat, or are making errant throws on the field. Yelling at them, calling them names, or getting angry at them only pollutes the team atmosphere. Most players know when they have screwed up. Having just a few chances each game to make an accurate throw or catch a fly ball means that blowing it on one of those occasions takes on a greater significance, especially if that blown chance leads to a loss. That's why baseball players need very short memories.

There would be so many opportunities to harbor anger during a season of baseball, between blown opportunities by teammates, unfair calls by umpires, and scathing press reports, that a player could get angry early and stay angry for a long time. As that player's health deteriorates, the team suffers and the air around him feels void of oxygen. To live in anger rather than to forgive would be totally forgetting the lesson of Little League, to marinate in affirmation. The angry, unforgiving person becomes the cancer infecting the larger whole. Hence, the need for immediate, generous, and continual forgiveness on the part of baseball players toward their teammates, umpires, fans, writers, and others.

Does this mean that you can never get angry at another person who makes a dumb choice, an errant throw, or mistake or who exhibits zero hustle at work, home, school, or on the field? Of course not! It may be your anger that alerts the person's attention to a bad habit that needs correcting. Your anger may jolt the person into recognizing their self-centeredness, allowing them to be more open to others. Your anger may precipitate an apology, which leads to healing. In all cases, however, letting go of anger is our assignment in that healing process, even if expressing it would compel someone else to change behavior or sweeten their language.

Mistakes will always occur as long as humans are human. Everyone blows it at some point in life with something. Our shame-based culture trains us to hide our vulnerabilities, blame others, and avoid taking responsibility for our mistakes. Forgiveness is often seen as capitulation, giving in to the other person, denying our feelings, or letting someone get away with their poor behavior, a sign of weakness. But what if we could practice a generosity of forgiveness? By recognizing that mistakes happen, giving people the benefit of the doubt (very few people intend to screw things up), and affirming one another we could keep alive that Little League atmosphere of affirmation where people flourish. Forgiving ourselves and forgiving others confirms our common humanity. We say yes to one another, even as we constantly disappoint one another.

A risk attends the person who forgives. In situations where trust is absent in a relationship, forgiving the other person only opens one up to disadvantage or even abuse. However, there is a certain gentleness that comes with forgiveness that allows people to be human, only human, and not pretend to be perfect or some kind of superhero. The long-haul season of baseball is a steady-state condition that makes it ripe for people to forgive generously, a condition necessary for strong relationships. There's an honesty to forgiving that admits people are good enough, not perfect. That's the language of baseball as well as healthy relationships. ♥

In the Batter's Box

Who do you need to forgive? Are you on that list? Are you recognizing the vulnerability, literally the humanity, of people, including yourself? What if you took the risk of letting go of your anger (or other feelings) and moved on with your life? What would you have to do or say to show up and dig in? How would you feel when you swing for the fences?

CHAPTER 21

THE BAT AS FRIEND OR FOE:
Decide Purposefully

$$\Diamond$$

Two beliefs are frequently held in tension and have a claim on our behavior. In the political realm, there are people who look at our human condition and place a premium on the belief that "we're all in it together." That is, we have a responsibility to care for others and to consider how our actions affect the larger human condition. Others assert that personal responsibility is the main guiding principle in life. Without relying on anyone else, we need to take care of ourselves. As logical constructs, both conditions are true and necessary. It's a "both-and" situation, not "either-or," for there are times when people need to shoulder personal responsibility just as there are times when we have to help others in need.

In counseling sessions over the years, I noticed some people would use their unfortunate childhood histories to maintain their victim status, excuse their bad behavior, and call into question their ability to change. Taking no personal responsibility for anything, they would wait for some person or situation to come along and rescue them. Conversely, there were people who simply found it too difficult to ask for help or to receive any kind of assistance. It was a sign of weakness to let others know that they couldn't do everything on their own. To live in healthy relationships, we need to be responsible for our words and actions, and we need to recognize that we need help from others from time to time. Both are true and necessary. It's up to us to decide how we'll live.

Some people rise above their tragic pasts, traumatic accidents, or deadly illnesses. They exhibit an inspiring resilience to adversity. They persevere persistently. They are open to any resource, tool, or help that others may provide. They also dig into what they need to do and simply do it. They control their attitudes and their efforts. Such people decide purposefully to hold competing claims in tension and swing for the fences. The tools and resources at hand become friends and useful allies in the quest for a better life or healthier relationships at home, work, or school.

A batter sometimes focuses on his slumping performance. He feels the weight of his team's ranking, as if it's all up to him whether they win or lose. Although he has Major League ability, he feels the disgrace of recent strikeouts, mistakes, and bad plays as he slumps to the plate. His bat holds the weight of past failures as it drills into his shoulder. His self-doubts and stinkin' thinkin' suck the energy out of his arms, rendering him virtually incapable of lifting the bat to swing.

As we've said, you can control your attitude and your effort. In this case, the bat is his foe, despite his having all the skill, knowledge, talent, and history of success that he needs in order to help his team win. There are no guarantees he'll get a hit if he swings. It's terribly difficult to do so. He will continue to guarantee failure, however, if he does NOT swing. That's why so many coaches tell their players, especially those in a slump, to swing anyway. They might just hit something.

Standing in the batter's box, the hitter's only tool is the bat. Sure, he can get closer to the plate or farther up in the batter's box, but all he has at his disposal is the bat. The pitcher has a few more tools. His basic tool is the ball, of course. But he can adjust the speed, angle, curve, and location of that tool using the skills and experience he has of throwing thousands of pitches over the years. Yet the batter's experience comes into play as well, and it is the batter's mindset that largely determines if all that experience, skill, and practice will be realized through the tool on his shoulder or be the anchor that ties him to failure.

Two equally talented, well-educated, and gifted students, each from difficult backgrounds, receive quality degrees from top-notch colleges. One continues to struggle in life, work, and relationships while the other rises to success in business and at home. The mindset of one is that of claiming the good, acknowledging the blessings she's received over the years, and shutting down the stinkin' thinkin' of the past, which could keep her trapped in defeat. The mindset of the other is still that of a victim. Harboring a sense of entitlement, he does not show up to life's challenges, and he does not dig into the tasks at hand, even though he is eminently qualified to handle those tasks. He fails to swing and to take a chance for fear of failure. He could also fear success. For then, he would have to drop the victim pretense and take responsibility for himself, no longer blaming others for any failure. One uses her past as a friend, propelling her to seize every available opportunity and giving thanks while the other uses his past as a foe to stay stuck emotionally, spiritually, or in other ways. ♥

In the Batter's Box

How about you? Are your life experiences a foe holding you back, or are they an impetus for you, like a friend, to use that life history as a helpful tool, creating the kind of life you really want? What could you do to break the stinkin' thinkin' that may be inhibiting you from swinging for the fences in your life? In what ways could you control your attitude and effort to change your mindset and take the bat of indifference, sloth, fear, or anger off your shoulder and swing for the fences at home, work, or school? Decide purposefully and then show up, dig in, and suck less.

CHAPTER 22

WINNING OR LOSING, IT'S ALL THE SAME:
Count Blessings

I worked with a guy who was preternaturally positive. He was so oddly positive that I wondered at times if he was mentally stable. He approached life the way he had approached his baseball career—all in. He loved playing ball every day. He loved getting his uniform filthy from sliding into base or diving for ground balls. Mastering the "baseball burrito," he would work that mess all game long (note: this is where a player makes bubble gum soft, takes it out of his mouth, pats it flat, puts in chewing tobacco, rolls it up, and puts it back in his mouth to chew and spit all afternoon). Being on the ball field, doing what he loved to do was a blessing for him. Winning or losing was important but not everything to him. Although he loved to win, a loss did not take away his love for the game or his desire to improve, to contribute, and to make his team a little better every day.

As a divinity school student in a hospital training program, I visited a woman confined to her bed. She had a tray crossing her bed on which someone could strap a book or notebook for her. The only movable part of her body was her head and mouth. She turned pages with a rubber-tipped stick. She was always bright and cheerful. Always. She talked of being a very active girl, young woman, and mother. The church to which she belonged for some eighty years was the center of her life. She used to "drive the little old ladies around," as she said, just a few short years ago. She wasn't sure why she was still so mentally active but so physically debilitated. "Maybe it's the only way God could get me to slow down," she joked at one point. With a working "ticker" (her brain), she figured she could still pray for people and situations. She asked me if I would add my name and the names of my family at the end of her current notebook. I thumbed through hundreds of lines of people and situations to find a blank line where I added my information and then turned back to the page she had been on. She smiled, gave thanks for being so blessed to be able to pray for me and my family, and asked if I could put her stick back into her mouth. With that, she gave me a wink and went back to her work of constant prayer. She had told me that she did not think she had a great deal of time to do this, given the rate of her decline, so she wanted to stay focused on the task at hand. I left, utterly overwhelmed by her spirit and her diligence.

Being in the game is a blessing all its own, whether it's literally a ball game or the game of life. As we saw earlier, a person's mindset has a great deal to do with her experience. Controlling attitude and effort is within the individual's ability. If we go into the game with a glass-half-full attitude, we are likely to experience the situation as positive and turn in a better performance. Approaching everything with a down-in-the-mouth, negative attitude spoils our relationships and tarnishes the moment. Again, stinkin' thinkin' gets in our way. Unless the situation is absolutely perfect, or the person totally flawless, our glass-half-empty thinking prevents us from counting any part a blessing.

Being positive and counting blessings does not mean someone is naive. Counting blessings in the midst of a crisis or natural disaster does not render one mentally unstable. Life, as with baseball, is a constant flow of good and bad, hope and despair, highs and lows. We tend to think of a good life or a good game as only the high point or the bright spot while minimizing the tough parts and the unkind or painful moments. This tendency allows us to savor victory and a game well played. Without the contrast, however, we would have no perspective. It's precisely because of the sore muscles, stained uniforms, broken hearts, disappointments, and failing bodies that a victory seems so uplifting. It's the reason why a woman in a hospital bed can still turn pages in her notebook with a rubber-tipped stick. The sum total is a blessing. Winning or losing, it's all the same. It's all a blessing. ❦

In the Batter's Box

It's easy to get caught up in the drive for perfection and winning, as if these are the only goals that matter. What would it be like to see participation as a goal in itself? How could you pull goodness from the moment and appreciate that just being present in a situation or in a relationship is a blessing in itself? In what ways could you count blessings whether you are winning or losing?

CHAPTER 23

DOING YOUR VERY BEST:
Cultivate Self-Esteem

We did not make the game. We lived hundreds of miles away. It was not possible in terms of schedules and timing to be present at our grandson's Little League game—the first one in his new neighborhood. I learned that the team had been badly defeated, the score just shy of the standard "skunk rule," where the game ends when the other side is ahead by more than ten runs with no chance of being defeated. I wasn't sure how he took the loss, so I asked gently on the phone how it went. "I did my very best, Papa," he proudly said. "That's what it's all about," I said in return. Such confidence and such self-esteem. I could not have been more proud.

Challenges, crises, and losses at work, in our home lives, or with loved ones can all deflate our self-esteem, which in turn can affect every facet of our lives. It happens to everyone. When it does, listen to your thoughts, especially your self-talk and how you interpret what's happening. Stinkin' thinkin' creeps in if we aren't vigilant. All-or-nothing thinking tries to convince us that if we fail at this task, then we're total losers. All we see is the negative and become convinced that others only see us in a negative light because of our mistakes. We convert something positive into something negative, as if our achievements don't count (it was too easy, we may say). Or we jump to a negative conclusion with no evidence to support it when a friend does not respond immediately to an email. Feeling like failures, we tell ourselves we are failures, confusing feelings with facts. Undervaluing ourselves, we are convinced that we don't deserve anything better. We spiral down into a morass of destructive self-talk, hobbling any attempt to create new possibilities or generate a new life. Once again, baseball comes to the rescue, especially the Little League culture of affirmation.

I watched the coach come to the mound. The thirteen-year-old pitcher was almost in tears. He had loaded the bases with poor pitching, including two walks. We know that everyone makes mistakes, but those mistakes don't make us bad people. However, he was obviously having a hard time getting out of his stinkin' thinkin'.' The coach came to the mound, looked around and said, "Look at this," indicating the field where they were playing in the Little League finals, "isn't it beautiful?" The coach acknowledged the tough situation but also that he had every confidence in the kid's ability. "Just throw strikes and put the ball in play," he told him. His team would back him up. The coach reminded him that he was one of the reasons why they had come this far in the tournament and that they had overcome tough situations all season long.

"So," he asked, "what do you want to do?"

"I want to get this guy," came the quick, solid reply.

"Then get him," the coach said, turning to head back to the dugout, "and let's have fun," he added as he patted the kid's back. The batter hit the next pitch into an inning-ending double play.

It's probably safe to say that other people and the situations we put ourselves in have as much, if not more, influence in shaping our sense of self-esteem than genetics or our "internal wiring" does. If someone is constantly put down, undervalued, and unappreciated at work, school, or home, that person shrivels up—perhaps even physically. It's also probably safe to say that we can't get rid of negative thoughts altogether. Instead of trying to fight them, or worse, being overwhelmed by them, accept them and feel them. Again, we're not looking for perfection, just for sucking less. Challenge the way you think about the negative thoughts. Ask, is this really true? How have I dealt with this situation before? What could I do to make this less stressful? Stop "shoulding" on yourself, making unreasonable demands on yourself or others. It's a way of creating more realistic expectations. In addition, treating yourself with kindness and encouragement can go a long way toward overcoming pessimism, which so often becomes a self-fulfilling prophecy. "Yes, this assignment could be tough, but I know I can handle it," is the antidote to your older brother's voice in your head, telling you that you suck. ♥

In the Batter's Box

Imagine you are that young pitcher on the mound in the championship game. You are on the edge of tears. You have put your team in a terrible position in part because of your poor performance. You may even have a work example or a situation with a spouse or friend that mimics this situation. Describe the "coach," the person who comes to you with affirmation, encouragement, and words of grace—the person who stands with you in this difficult moment and asks you what you want to do . . . then tells you to have fun. Who is that person? How could you be that person to yourself, if you can't name someone? How do you feel after that conversation?

CHAPTER 24

BASEBALL IS TIMELESS:
Stop Rushing

There are no clocks in baseball. You can call a time-out at any point when you're in the batter's box. Take as much time as you need. The pitch count is four balls and three strikes. However, you can keep batting after two foul balls as long as you keep hitting the ball. I once heard of a batter getting more than twenty foul balls during one at bat. Imagine that! That would be like pitching a couple of normal innings just to a single batter! And there are no "tied games" in baseball. You have to play until one team wins. Extra-inning games are a lot of fun for baseball enthusiasts, especially if you have great seats. Scoring could be a challenge, however, since most scorebooks only have columns for a few extra innings. There have been games that have gone seventeen innings and more, which is like a doubleheader with no break. Rain delays can last a couple of hours, making everyone wait until it's safe to go back on the field. In cold-weather cities, there have even been snow delays. Perhaps the shortest game in history was on September 28, 1919 when the New York Giants beat the Philadelphia Phillies in fifty-one minutes.

If individual games are not bound by physical time, the game itself has been a part of our nation's history for so long that it's hard to imagine when we were not playing baseball. Although some aspects of the game have changed, and the equipment has certainly improved over the years (think batting helmets), we play the game with almost the same stuff that we did a century ago. Fans may not dress up as they did years ago, wearing suits and ties, but they still come with all the same enthusiasm and anticipation as their parents and grandparents before them. So much has changed in our society that I often hear people say while commenting on baseball that it's the one thing that has remained constant in their lives. It's timeless, in more ways than one.

"Time is money," the saying goes. We have all kinds of executive training sessions that show us how to manage our time more efficiently so that we can be more productive. If we look at it another way, that's how companies can get more out of us for less money. For centuries in this country, being unproductive (as in not working constantly) or lazy has drawn criticism and scorn. In our society, we are obsessed with time. We want things to happen quickly. We have difficulty sitting still for any length of time. Educators have noticed that children's attention spans seem to be decreasing from previous generations. Many people bemoan the fact that kids spend so much time in front of screens, playing video games or watching movies, and less time reading or playing outside, and that they have a hard time just being still in the present moment. The constant barrage of images creates a state of hypersensitivity, perhaps even anxiety, whereby quiet time, relaxing time, and downtime are viewed in a negative light.

Rather than shun baseball as boring or too slow, I suggest that it's high time we recultivate our love of the game. In so doing, we regain the ability to relax into the moment. We don't have to hurry anywhere. There is nothing we have to accomplish right now. We can simply be present with our friends, families, neighbors, and ourselves. Sit. Quietly. Having no agenda, no SMART goals, no process improvements, and no assignments, we can just be still. To help our focus, we could keep score. But we could also just visit with our neighbors and enjoy the pitching, hitting, and fielding of the game in front of us.

Being still is a spiritual discipline. All the great mystics and religious leaders through the ages have taught their disciples that the first step in strengthening one's relationship with the Divine is being still, being quiet, and not rushing. Baseball could do more for you than simply lower your blood pressure. It could nurture your spiritual well-being!

All too often, I hear people complaining that they don't have enough time. They don't have time to do the things they want to do. They don't have time to spend with family and friends the way they desire. They talk about rushing from this thing to that, driving kids here and there, cramming in work activities and travel, to the point where they often say, "There just aren't enough hours in the day!" Their recreation encompasses loud, raucous activity and even violent sports, with ever-changing, time-sensitive movements often accompanied by even more stress and tension affecting their emotional health. With no time for quiet, no time for introspection, and no time for slowing down, people drive themselves to exhaustion . . . and start all over again—the same rat race tomorrow. Like the hamster running in its wheel, there is seemingly no end to the rushing.

Baseball can fix that. There is the excitement surrounding a game, especially during playoffs. There are stressful moments, such as when the bases are loaded with two outs in the bottom of the ninth, and you're down three runs. The swiftness of a well-executed double play creates a flurry of activity not unlike certain ballet moves. These are measured stresses, but not constant. One simply unplugs when coming to a baseball game. Rushing, driving, relentless screaming, and unceasing chaos have no place at a baseball game (except at maybe the seventh game of the World Series). It's a pastoral sport, played in a park or on a field. You can be as involved as you want to be, such as tracking pitches and keeping score, or simply relaxing and talking with those around you. Try it the next time you feel out of control with the world spinning around you. Go to a baseball game and relax. ❦

In the Batter's Box

Imagine going to a baseball game as a way to slow down, enter into a state of timelessness, and relax into the moment. Does that sound appealing or does it make you nervous? Are you willing to try it? Would it help you to keep score, as a way to give you something to do while you relax? In what ways is that baseball experience different from your everyday life?

CHAPTER 25

THE POSTSEASON AS A "DO-OVER":
Celebrate Opportunity

It was a provocative statement. It made me think. The speaker was a therapist who worked with adults who had suffered various traumas and abuse in the past. She said that it is never too late to have a happy childhood. Never too late to have a happy childhood . . . What does that mean exactly? Should we act like kids? Are we to shirk our current obligations as parents, employees, and spouses? I could see other people nodding their heads, agreeing with her statement. It seemed to resonate with everyone in the room. What she was talking about was indeed provocative, but not impossible.

I would be too self-conscious to get on a swing at the park by myself or to jump on a merry-go-round with a bunch of kids. I might also get beat up by their parents. However, doing these activities with my grandchildren is another story. "Look at that old guy, playing with his grandkids!" people now say. All of a sudden, it's acceptable as well as fun. We can run all over the jungle gym, with them as "prey" and me as "monster," laughing and shrieking with no one calling the cops. Playing make-believe, throwing batting practice, paddling a kayak, skating, riding an inner tube down a snowy hill, splashing in the water, and doing a thousand and one things that children do every day are all opportunities to relive childhood. Interacting in healthy ways, across generations, is one way to have a happy childhood and be blessed with a "do-over."

Baseball's "second season," as some people have referred to the playoffs, is an opportunity for another chance. Perhaps the team finished first in the division, clearly outstanding through the long-haul season. Perhaps the team finished close enough (good baseball philosophy) to have a run at a wild card playoff spot. Either way, all teams start at zero during the postseason. It's happened before—some guy who has a handful of home runs during the regular season and who is not at all known as a power hitter suddenly comes alive and hits as many home runs in the postseason as he did since last April. Don Larsen, not known as a particularly outstanding pitcher, to this day has the only perfect game ever thrown in the World Series.

We love second chances. We love it when people strive hard, work hard, fail, and then pick themselves up and go at it again. There's something about a never-say-die attitude that is inspiring. With baseball, that second-chance opportunity is built into the postseason. A team that is not known for especially hot hitting or consistent pitching nevertheless makes it to the brackets leading to the World Series. Everyone pulls out their best Little League affirmation, encourages one another, has fun, and jumps at opportunities. On defense, players stretch, dive, and run just a little bit more. On offense, they swing for the fences, steal bases, and suck a little less than a few months before. The fans get into it, and the emotions feed into a virtuous cycle of excitement. Win or lose, it's rewarding to see everyone having so much fun.

I've had managers who would let no mistake, no matter how insignificant or inconsequential, go unnoticed or unpunished. The morale of the work team was a life-draining, toxic environment. Everyone found other employment in record time. I've also had situations where a certain grace prevailed. Mistakes were acknowledged and corrected, perhaps even consequences shared, but business moved forward in life-enhancing ways. "Do-overs" were part of the learning process and improvement naturally followed.

Key relationships in our lives are replete with opportunities to "do it again." We are ever-evolving as people and more so in relationships. What used to work in our relationships before might not work in the future. For example, learning how to share feelings makes it difficult if not impossible to clam up in a conversation with one's spouse. Conversations are always ongoing. We can revisit an unpleasant exchange with someone simply by saying that we would like to say more about that conversation. We can add new insight, an "aha," a feeling, or a deeper understanding of what the conversation was about. We can ask for clarifying statements. With trust and respect between people, we can revisit just about anything, keeping at it until all parties are satisfied. Like baseball, we show up, dig in, and suck less as we swing for the fences in strengthening our relationships, feeling grateful for second chances. ♥

In the Batter's Box

Are there conversations you want to revisit with someone? What would you say? How could you say it in a way that he or she would re-engage in the conversation? If you are around children, in what ways could you enjoy a happy childhood, whether as a reminder of what you had or as a way of capturing what was never present? Where are the "do-over" moments at work, with managers or direct reports?

CHAPTER 26

COACH'S CORNER:
Banish Shame

Shame is so pervasive in our culture, and so toxic, that it's time we banish it altogether. Baseball is our antidote. The life lessons we glean from baseball can heal us, individually and collectively, as we put them to use. One of the hallmarks of shame is that we constantly focus on failure and defects (ours and those of others around us). Over the years, as we reinforce our self-insulting thoughts, shame colors everything we do and say. Even when we receive praise or recognition, we explain it away as something we didn't deserve, as something they didn't really mean, or as something that was so easy that anyone could've won. In interpersonal relationships, it's easy to see why shame can be so destructive, especially if two people struggle with lingering toxicity from the past. Seeing everything in a negative light and harboring rigid rules about how people should behave makes it easy to find fault in others and to judge them accordingly. We try to escape from these self-defeating thoughts by focusing on the worst in people and in situations, and we relive our mistakes over and over again.

Baseball is the antidote to shame. It offers us healing. New ways of thinking about ourselves, living in relationships with others, and working together to solve difficult problems facing our society are all made possible through baseball. Showing up to the situation in front of us, digging into the tasks at hand, sucking less, and doing our very best because others are counting on us allows us to swing for the fences and realize outcomes we never thought possible.

Perfection is impossible. Controlling our attitudes and our efforts will enable us to improve our relationship skills over time. We'll become better at tasks that demand focused attention. We'll stop being held hostage by our emotions and recognize that the universe is not against us, life happens, and we are stronger together.

Challenging negative thinking is what good coaches do with their players. A batter begins to do some stinkin' thinkin' about his ability to hit. His coach challenges him to articulate how he is so certain that he will fail. He asks the batter for evidence, especially to compare evidence from the hitting streak he enjoyed just a few weeks ago. What's keeping the hitter from letting go of this current thought? Perhaps it's time to look at videos from recent at bats. Maybe there's an issue around not extending his arms, twisting his hips at the wrong time, or pulling his head up, or a thousand other small things that he could do to improve his swing with practice, practice, practice. Finally it's not just about the hitter. It's about the team. People are counting on him to show up, dig in, and suck less. He can't guarantee success by swinging, but he can certainly lock in failure by not doing so. Bottom line: swing for the fences.

Baseball is at once incredibly simple and yet so profound. Because it has been a part of our national pastime for so long, it has integrated itself into our subconscious. We know that Little League affirmation is the best way to strengthen relationships and to build effective teams. Hope endures no matter what, and we want to believe in new beginnings. The long-haul season we experience in marriage, work, or school requires us to focus on the present moment instead of lingering on past mistakes. We need to forgive, respect one another, and take risks. We can be open to new ideas and willing to try new things, use our gifts and talents for the good of the whole, and be grateful. Practicing baseball etiquette and challenging our stinkin' thinkin' banishes shame and its toxic effects from our lives. Deciding to work together could cause us to "reclaim the commons," those things in life that belong to us all, from our environment to our democracy to our way of life. We won't be perfect, but we will begin to suck less.

Good coaches are not likely to spend a great deal of time psychoanalyzing their players. If someone is in a slump and gets tangled up in his stinkin' thinkin,' the coach is probably going to require more time in the batting cage under supervision. One of the most effective ways of cutting off stinkin' thinkin' is to block it with focused attention elsewhere. Baseball gives us that important life lesson. So when we're tangled up with negative self-talk about relationships at work, home, or school, or when we tend to discount our accomplishments, we can do ourselves a great favor by diligently focusing our attention on something else. Like baseball. In the next chapter, we'll take a look at how scoring could be exactly the focusing tool that we have been seeking for a long time. With a few simple techniques, we could be well on our way to healing and new life! ♥

In the Batter's Box

There are various mechanisms, therapies, techniques, and tools that people have used over the years to help others overcome the pervasive toxicity of shame. The Hazelden Betty Ford Foundation based in Center City, Minnesota, has a number of books and publications around the issue of shame and its effects on people and relationships (see hazelden.org). There are many other centers and therapists across the country who can help as well. Please research some of these resources. Take a moment to reflect on your learning, perhaps even jotting down some notes. We need you back in the game of life, focused and swinging for the fences.

CHAPTER 27

BALLS, STRIKES, HITS, AND RUNS:
Keep Score

Why keep score? So often in our everyday lives we encounter others keeping score, especially when it comes to us. They are remembering small slights, intended or by accident. They judge our behavior by some internal gauge and often find us deficient. No matter what we say or do, there are some people we simply cannot please. Rather than giving in to that type of scorekeeping, however, let's turn our focus to scoring baseball, which will direct our attention away from toxic, shaming situations toward the life-affirming world of baseball.

There are different types of scorebooks, but the ones I like have a spiral binding on the short side of a rectangle and a heavy cardboard cover. They lay across my lap and are stiff enough for me to write on (and erase, on occasion). My family and I write short journal entries in the margins of our scorebooks. We have excerpts from our lives recorded throughout the years. One can literally see the history of our family through the lens of baseball. When our son announced his engagement to our daughter-in-law, we wrote it in the margin of a game between the Minnesota Twins and the Kansas City Royals. Weather, news headlines, political campaigns, and family events ride along the pages, which detail pitch counts, runs scored, and batting orders. We have woven together a tapestry of stories, connecting our lives with an energy and history much larger than just us. Looking back, I can see that we are but a small part in a much larger picture, even as that picture helps define who and what we are. Over the long-haul season of our lives together, we have learned how to be coachable, to adapt, and not to sweat the small stuff. Forgiving, affirming, and encouraging one another, we keep swinging, never guaranteeing success but staving off failure. At least we're in this together. As time has elapsed, we realize just how much we need our family and our friends to make it to the postseason and beyond.

Henry Chadwick, a British writer, is credited with inventing the first box score in the 1850s, before the Civil War, more than a century and a half ago. I see it as an art form, tracking not only pitching and batting duals, but also the beauty of highlight-reel-worthy defense. To keep a box score is to be part of a century-old art form. Kelsey McKinney, a writer for *Fusion*, was quoted in the New York Times as saying that it's hard to enjoy baseball if you don't know what you're looking for, and that it's the box score that teaches us just how to do that—to look. Watching carefully and tuning out distractions, something we've discussed in previous chapters, doesn't seem to fit very well with a lot of people these days. That's too bad.

I am encouraged, however, whenever I go to the ballpark. I see men, women, and children all looking, paying attention, and keeping score. I'd love to see more, but this little band of scorekeepers is alive and well. We smile and give a knowing nod when we see each other's books. It's fun to talk to people and look at how they do things. Do they fill in the little diamonds on their sheets when a runner scores? Or do they even have little diamonds on their sheets? I put a backward "K" in the box when a batter takes a called third strike. Once, I saw a guy put an exclamation point after his backward "K" to convey a really good pitch.

When my daughter was a little girl, she looked at our scorebook during a game, shaking her head at the pitch count. She said that the pitcher was working too hard. After all, the batter was only hitting a buck-eighty-five and had struck out his last two at bats. I asked her what she would do as the pitcher. "I'd waste something. Throw it low and away," she said sternly. "He'd probably just chase it anyway. Worst that could happen is that he'd hit a ground ball for an easy out." The man sitting a few seats away from us looked stunned. I patted my chest and mouthed the words, "my girl." Surely, as proud a moment with her as I've ever had.

Years later, at another game, I asked her how long we had been scoring games. At that point, it had been more than a decade. "Wow," I said, "that's a lot of baseball." She reached over, touched my arm, and said, "A lot of good times, Dad."

As you keep your scorebook, focus on what's in front of you. Journal some current events in the margins, and you will bring order to your otherwise chaotic and stress-filled life. You will track successes as well as mistakes, noticing that lots of little things players do as a team add up to winning. No one will be perfect. And you will have a written record, a history, of slowing down and paying attention in a timeless setting. This process can be a sacred healing exercise to rid yourself of the toxic shame that permeates our culture. ❦

In the Batter's Box

Next time you are in front of a computer, go to "Using a Baseball Scorecard with Greg Bancroft" on YouTube. It is a plug for my children's book, *Betsy's Day at the Game,* where a little girl goes to a baseball game with her grandfather and keeps score. The reader learns how to keep score and can practice at the end of the book. For those of you unfamiliar with the art of scoring, you might find this helpful as you enjoy the game of baseball.

Additionally, I would hope that keeping a box score would trigger healthy thoughts on ways to strengthen your daily life and relationships with others at home, work, or school, helping you to enjoy more fully the game of life.